Stories with a Purpose

Stories with a Purpose

Lessons for the Spirit, Lessons for the Heart

Ronnie J. Muro
Rosanna P. Tsivourakis

Saint Mary's Press®

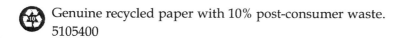 Genuine recycled paper with 10% post-consumer waste.
5105400

The publishing team included Laurie Delgatto, development editor; Lorraine Kilmartin, reviewer; prepress and manufacturing coordinated by the prepublication and production services departments of Saint Mary's Press.

Printed in the United States of America

Printing: 9 8 7 6 5 4 3 2

Year: 2014 13 12 11 10 09 08 07 06

ISBN-13: 978-0-88489-659-3
ISBN-10: 0-88489-659-5

Library of Congress Cataloging-in-Publication Data
Muro, Ronnie J.
        Stories with a purpose : lessons for the spirit, lessons for the heart / Ronnie J. Muro and Rosanna P. Tsivourakis.
        p. cm.
ISBN 0-88489-659-5 (pbk.)
        1. Storytelling in Christian education. 2. Christian education of young people. 3. Catholic Church—Education. I. Tsivourakis, Rosanna P. II. Title.

BX926.3.M87 2006

268'.6—dc21

                                                                2005018297

Dedications

To my parents, for their example; my family, for their love; and the young people in my community, for their inspiration.

— Ronnie Muro

To my parents, whose stories gave me my identity; to my brothers and sister, who live the stories with me; to Baki, Niko, Aleka, Pia, and Erica, my own beloved storytellers, in whom I delight.

— Rosanna Tsivourakis

Authors' Acknowledgments

Thank you to all who allowed me to share my stories and encouraged me to continue sharing them.

Thank you to my wife, Debbie, for her love, undying support, and endless patience.

Thank you to Chris, my son and best friend, for writing so many new chapters in my life; to Natalie, my precious daughter, for filling my heart with more love than I knew possible; and to Natalie's husband, Josh, for enriching our family story.

Thank you to my parents for their great example of love and family—Daddy, the greatest storyteller of all, and Mama, who still inspires me. I miss you both.

Thank you to all members, past and present, of Saint Patrick Catholic Church in Adamsville, Alabama, especially the young people of SPIRIT and the fellow adult leaders who lived the stories with me.

Thank you to Sr. Joan Harrington and Fr. Ray Murrin for giving me the opportunity to minister to young people.

Thank you to Laurie for showing confidence in me and for helping make a dream come true.

Thank you, God, for blessing me with my faith, my family, my church. Without you, I am nothing.

—Ronnie Muro

Thanks to Pia and Erica for not griping when I monopolized the family computer, and to my husband for his quiet smile of acknowledgment that, yeah, I could do this.

Thanks to family and friends who were interested enough to keep me on the ball; to G, who always said I should do this; to Renay, whose memory of my story was better than my own; and to Laurie Ann, ever the good friend, the encourager, the drill sergeant.

—Rosanna Tsivourakis

Contents

Preface. 11

Foreword. 13

Introduction 15

Chapter 1
Old Spice 21

Chapter 2
Feeding the Hunger 29

Chapter 3
Thanksgiving Touchdowns 35

Chapter 4
The Search 41

Chapter 5
Sight 49

Chapter 6
Hanging Out on the Fringe. 57

Chapter 7
Mom Was Right 65

Chapter 8
The Stick 73

Chapter 9
The Hike 81

Chapter 10
Caller ID 87

Chapter 11
The Stick Lives On 95

Chapter 12
A Seat on the Bus 103

Chapter 13
The Orange Drink 109

Chapter 14
A Miracle 117

Acknowledgments 125

Preface

When I was a child, my dad told me stories of superheroes saving the world or animals that were able to talk to me only. Now as an adult, I hear stories of other people's childhood memories or the current news of the day. Most of the time, these stories are not as exciting as talking animals, but not much is.

My father has told and written thousands of stories throughout the years. The stories he has chosen to share in this book are not the same ones I heard as a child. These are true stories of his life, our life. At the time, I saw these events as simple everyday occurrences, as nothing exciting, and certainly not as lessons to be learned. After an event, my father would share with me his version of what had happened, allowing me to see it through his eyes. Through his storytelling, my dad managed to teach me valuable lessons at the most unexpected of times.

My father and Rosanna have adapted their stories into a format to help illustrate lessons. The lessons vary from topics like self-confidence to friendship. I encourage you to read these stories to the young people you lead, read the Bible passages associated with each, and invite the participants to reflect on how each story may relate to their life and how they can use what they have learned to make a difference.

Sharing a story with someone is a gift. The stories we tell and the stories we hear become a part of who we are: they link us to the past or propel us toward the future. The ability to truly listen to another's story allows each of us the wonderful opportunity to see life, ever so briefly, through someone else's eyes.

—Christopher J. Muro

Foreword

The theme of this book, the importance of storytelling, reminds me of an event in my youth that inspired me to be a teacher. I was fortunate enough to be placed in some advanced English classes while in high school. I say fortunate not for the accelerated curriculum but for the teacher, Ms. Dale Quin, who would instruct me for three years. She was a small, nearly weathered, gruff woman who, at all costs, did her best to conceal her tenderness. She succeeded. Most of us thought she was too hard, too insensitive, and too mean. Ah, the wonders of appearance versus reality! Her class was certainly structured, often overly demanding (for which I am thankful now), and required full participation. Grades fell swiftly for those who sat idle. She demanded our best efforts. She facilitated a dynamic classroom — a community — and slowly my classmates and I began to realize that a transformation was happening within us.

One day toward the end of my junior year, we entered class at the bell's beckoning. I noticed that Ms. Quin seemed different, distressed. The impetus for what followed remains a mystery to me. She pulled a chair out to roughly the center of the room — a small, humble chair that seemed the perfect accompaniment for what transpired. She sat. She began to speak. What poured forth was a moment of story sharing that changed the way we perceived her. This titan began to shrink; her humanity brought her down to us. A throne may have seemed more appropriate the day before, but this day the wooden chair suited her perfectly.

She was compelled, she said, to reveal certain aspects of her personal story that may or may not clarify certain aspects of her classroom persona. She told us, slowly, of her introversion as a child and of the sanctuary she found in stories and words. Following her own education, she felt called to re-enter the field, but from the opposite perspective. She wanted to share the richness of the word with others. And there was more.

She told of medical complications that prevented her from ever having children. As she told of her condition and how she learned to cope by "adopting" her students, each of us felt the sublimity of the moment. She told us that she had the good fortune of getting to know us, of having us in class for a few years, of forming relationships. She invested her energy in us because we were her children. In that very moment, the governance and administration of the classroom suddenly made sense to me. The moments of heightened anger or joy, of extreme pressure or deep discussion happened as they would in a living room with one's family. I realized that Ms. Quin's behavior was justified because she loved us and thus expected of us that which she might have expected from her own children. I was overwhelmed. Needless to say, the remainder of our time with her was fruitful, energetic, often loud, and always healthy! This great mother of the classroom suddenly got the best from all her students.

It was the sharing, the willingness to shatter the arbitrary and necessary divisions, that lured us. In Ms. Quin's vulnerable moment, she appeared to us as monumentally strong. And the reciprocation, I think, validates the sharing. Her sharing was replete with virtues. Her time with us was laden with those best qualities of love that are described in 1 Corinthians 13: "Love is patient; love is kind; love is not envious or boastful or arrogant or rude. It does not insist on its own way; it is not irritable or resentful; it does not rejoice in wrongdoing, but rejoices in the truth" (vv. 4–6).

This brave woman, who was willing to lovingly share her story, compelled us to be better students.

Stories with a Purpose: Lessons for the Spirit, Lessons for the Heart offers a variety of personal stories, each uniquely replete with its own virtues. Each is a small instance of sharing, from the author to you and the young people you lead. The stories have a transformative power. They propagate all that is good and worth keeping and act as a catalyst for positive change. As was evidenced by Ms. Quin's honest sharing with us, there is an invaluable reciprocal value to telling a story.

—Niko Tsivourakis, graduate student of education,
University of Alabama at Birmingham

Introduction

The Power of Storytelling

We are all storytellers. Rarely can we get through a normal day without telling or hearing a story or two. By telling stories, we entertain and inform, but we also grow in self-understanding. Yet in this electronic age, the wonder and enjoyment of reading or listening to a good story is often lost to the lure of the Internet, interactive DVDs, video games, and cable television. It is difficult to compete with the glamour of media, whose activities are frequently solo endeavors, removing a young person from the company of peers and family. Media is mechanically driven, precluding the need for the viewer or listener to have an imagination or communication skills. Storytelling, on the other hand, fosters the ability and desire to use both the imagination and communication skills to build and support relationships. One would wonder, then, how media entertainment could compete with the more personal give-and-take of sharing stories with one another. . . .

Storytelling has become more difficult. Attention spans are shorter, more demanding, and more sophisticated. Perhaps it is the sharp contrast between sensory overload and the quiet enjoyment of simply listening that makes young people pay attention when stories are presented. In this way, storytelling is a unique teaching tool for illustrating lessons of moral value.

Most dictionaries define *story* as a narrative account of real or imagined events. We use stories to pass on accumulated wisdom, beliefs, and values. We explain how things are, why they are, and our role and purpose in life. Stories are the building blocks of knowledge, the foundation of memory and learning. Stories connect us with our humanness and link the past, the present, and the future by teaching us to anticipate the possible consequences of our actions.

Matters of faith also lend themselves to storytelling. Jesus knew the power of stories and often used parables as a way to connect with people and teach them. Carefully choosing images familiar to his audience, Jesus presented clear and simple examples to illustrate his lessons. The sower, the vineyard, and the mustard seed were familiar images to those who worked the land.

Jesus knew, as do all good storytellers, that stories stimulate listeners and open them up to a fuller experience of learning. Rather than merely hearing a lesson dictated to them, when people listen to a story, they experience emotion, create visual images, and process the story's message on multiple levels. This leads to a deeper understanding of what the story is trying to convey. More than any other form of communication, storytelling is an essential part of the human experience.

How to Use This Book

An Overview

Our daily routine is filled with seemingly meaningless events, but when we are aware of God's hand, the events take on new meaning. Each story in this book delivers a message about living the Christian life. The settings, circumstances, and themes vary, but the fundamental message is that God is working in our lives today.

Telling the Story

As the storyteller, you will need to be well prepared in order to have success with your listeners. The most effective stories are those told by people who have obvious excitement and passion for their stories. That is the lure that captures the attention of the listeners and holds their interest. When you love the story, your listeners will respond.

Once you settle on a story, spend time with it. You may need to tell it a few times before you feel completely comfortable with it. Here are some tips for getting to know your story:

- Read the story several times, first for pleasure, then with concentration.
- Analyze the appeal of the story—the word pictures you want your listeners to see and the mood you wish to create.
- Live with your story until the characters and setting become as real to you as people and places you know.
- Visualize it! Imagine sounds, tastes, scents, colors. Only when you know the story sensually can you convey the images to your audience.
- Learn the story as a whole rather than in fragments. Master the structure of the story and then simplify it to a basic outline of scenes. Do not try to memorize it.
- Practice the story often—in front of the mirror, to your cat, while you're driving in the car, with friends, or with anyone who will listen. Even when

telling an old and familiar story, you must use imagination and skill to make it come alive.

As you relate the story, speak with confidence and emotion. Use your voice, facial expressions, gestures, and body language to help deliver the story. Pause for emphasis when appropriate, and vary the pace of your telling. For instance, if you are speaking of a frantic time, speak rapidly to capture the emotion. Let your voice convey the emotion not only by your tone and inflection, but by your pace and rhythm. Facial expressions can add to the visualization of the story, but make sure they are natural and appropriate. Do not exaggerate them so much that they distract from the story.

Practice your delivery so that it becomes natural. Becoming totally familiar with the story will allow you to know the proper time to pause, speed up, alter your voice pattern, or use facial expressions. All these elements combine to make a story effective and interesting.

If you have not had time to become completely familiar with the story, you will need a copy in front of you. You may choose to read the whole story or just parts of it. Reading certain sections word for word will bring emphasis to those sections. You may decide to switch back and forth from paraphrasing the story and reading excerpts. Whatever your method, speak clearly, with emotion and purpose. Continue to engage your audience by maintaining as much eye contact as possible if you are reading.

Breaking Open the Story

Allowing time for the listeners to reflect on and discuss the story is a necessary part of storytelling. Therefore, each chapter includes a set of discussion and reflection questions, group activity ideas, and a prayer experience to help the participants take a deeper look at the message, moral, or purpose of the story and relate it to their own lives. You can use the discussion and reflection questions in large or small group settings, or you can offer them for individual reflection.

You can use the activities with the group to further process the story. The activities will help active learners see the lessons more clearly, as the participants will be able to "touch" and "feel" them by participating in some physical and mental processes. Some activities require preparation, so be sure you review them thoroughly ahead of time to determine which work best for you and your group.

An important part of the lesson is living the story—carrying out its message. Examples of how to live the message of each story are offered, and you may

choose to share those ideas with the group. Each suggestion calls the participants to action, inviting them to do something positive. A great story will do
more than entertain; it will change its listeners. By taking an action based on the
story's lesson, the participants are changed and, more important, so is the world.

The prayer experience that ends each chapter is geared to complete the communication of the story, the discussion and reflection, and the challenge to live
the story. The stories show how God is present to us in our everyday lives and
how God's lessons are often taught in the most mundane situations and ordinary times. Prayer is an invitation for the group to ask for God's guidance and
companionship on this journey. Prayer also reminds us of our dependence on
God and the hope that we continue to be mindful of God's presence in our daily
lives.

A Final Note from the Authors

Storytelling works! We all have a desire to be connected with others. We do this
best when we allow ourselves the freedom to be vulnerable to one another as we
explore the experiences we share. These are *our* stories. Both of us have told
them and retold them as a way of expressing emotion, sharing a lesson learned,
or connecting with new friends. It is our hope that as you read them and prepare to use them, you will find as much value in them as we do.

But don't stop with these stories. Find your own voice to tell the stories that
have shaped and influenced *your* life. Tell the stories that have stayed with you
as you have grown and matured — the stories that are the red flags of your con-
science, waving wildly whenever you need help making a decision or whenever
you feel confused.

Tell the stories of your families. Begin now to record what you know of the
members of your families, especially the elders and those who have passed on.
Reflect on what you have learned from family members and how you can pass
that wisdom on. Share these stories with the next generation so that they also
may become a part of the stories.

Tell the stories of your friends. What have you learned in life from others
around you? Childhood is filled with one adventure after another, but it is only
after some reflection that we find the significance of some of these events. What
friends, events, or situations in your life helped shape the person you have
become? Share those lessons with others.

Tell the stories of your faith. How have you struggled along your journey?
Who or what helped you along the way to keep the faith? Share what you

learned from your struggles and your successes to help show the way for others. Often the simplest of stories contain a deeper message, one that God has placed there for you. Perhaps that message changed your life without you even knowing it. Share that message with others so that they too can be changed. Then ask them to pass their stories on as well. Many of us want to make a difference in the world. We can do that one person at a time, one story at a time.

Chapter 1
Old Spice

Key Themes

- It is better to give than to receive.
- We should all share our gifts and talents with others.
- Selfishness can keep us from seeing the bigger picture.
- Seeing things from another perspective often causes a change of heart.

Scripture Connections

- Matthew 2:7–12 (The Magi presented Jesus with gifts.)
- Matthew 25:14–30 (Use your gifts wisely.)
- Romans 12:6–8 (We all have different gifts.)
- 1 Corinthians 12:4–31 (We all have different gifts, but they are given by the same Spirit.)

The Story

Offer the following introduction before telling the story:

  o   In this story, a son's love for his father is challenged by his hurt at having his gift rejected. But love prevails, and through time the son realizes his father's actions might have had a different motivation.

Each Christmas Eve, my three brothers and I, along with our younger sister, would nervously wait on Mama and Daddy to get home from work so we could open our presents. This particular year, I was especially excited because I had bought gifts for everyone in the family with my own money. That was no small task, as I was of limited income, to say the least, and ours was quite a large family. But I saved and guarded my precious coins and dollar bills all year so I could go Christmas shopping.

My shopping spree usually occurred at the nearest drug store where I could find a variety of reasonably priced items. I would carefully look at the handkerchiefs, ties, wallets, puzzle books, perfume, and toys, looking for just the right gift for each person. In spite of the great effort (and sizeable funds) that went into my gifts, they rarely got the appreciation they deserved. But, no matter, it is better to give than to receive, and I loved buying Christmas gifts.

This year I bought a bottle of Old Spice for Daddy. The box it came in made a great-looking gift, and it was a perfect size for wrapping. It was just one of the many gifts opened that Christmas Eve that found its way to my father's stack of presents. When we were finished opening all the presents, my brothers, sister, and I headed to the next order of business—our baths. That was followed by the annual tradition of putting on the new pajamas we had just received and waiting for Santa's arrival later that night.

Just after our baths, our neighbor from across the street stopped in. Mr. Holley was not our favorite neighbor. Maybe it was because of the time our ball rolled into his yard and he threatened to whip us, or maybe it was because of his foul disposition and the way he seemed to dislike kids. Either way, I stayed in the back of the house to avoid him.

After some time, I heard the conversation wrapping up and peered in from the hall to make sure he was leaving. To my horror, I heard Mr. Holley say as he headed for the door, "Well, if I don't get anything else for Christmas, at least I can say I got some aftershave!"

There in his hand—Mr. Holley's hand—was the Old Spice I had given to my father! I could not believe my eyes. I ran to my room and curled up, crying like a baby. How could Daddy give away the gift I had just given him? I was crushed. Okay, maybe it was a bad gift, but I picked it out myself. I paid for it myself! I just could not believe it.

My three brothers, in their best sympathetic fashion, immediately began laughing at me. They thought it was hilarious—first that it would happen and second that I would cry about it. Not surprisingly, Mama came to my room and tried to explain. Of course she's going to take Daddy's side, I thought to myself. She explained that Mr. Holley would not be getting any presents this Christmas. (Now there's a surprise, I thought.) Mama told me Daddy felt sorry for him and wanted him to have something this Christmas, so he gave him the aftershave. Of course, I asked why Daddy couldn't have given Mr. Holley something else, but I never did get a satisfactory answer.

Thanks to Santa's generosity, thoughts of aftershave were a million miles away as I awoke the next morning to a room full of toys and games. After hours of playing, we all had to get dressed and leave our toys behind. The entire family was to gather at my grandfather's house for Christmas dinner.

When we arrived at Poppa's house, we began the typical family exchange of gifts. One of those gifts was a plain white dress shirt that my parents had brought to give to my uncle Tony, the youngest of my father's brothers. Uncle Tony was a little troubled this Christmas, I suppose, as he watched Poppa open gifts from his family. Uncle Tony had never gotten around to doing his own Christmas shopping this year, so when he received the gift from my parents, he immediately took the shirt, stuck a twenty dollar bill in the wrapper, and handed it right over to Poppa! Naturally my parents were outraged. How could he do that? It was just not right for him to give Poppa the gift we had just given him.

Thus was the conversation as we drove home. Huddled in the back seat, I listened quietly for a while. My courage grew, and I finally spoke up: "It's just like the Old Spice. Daddy gave my gift away, and you told me that was okay. What's so bad about Uncle Tony giving the shirt away?"

"This is different," came the reply from the front seat. Different. Yeah, right. No, it's the same thing, I thought. Now they knew how it felt. I kept quiet, thinking that somehow justice had been served. Just one day removed from the great aftershave incident, the culprit, my father, had been dealt a cruel ironic blow. How sweet it was!

Of course, I eventually got over the hurt of that day, although my brothers will tell you that I complained about it well into my adulthood. I finally was able to see the story a little differently. Yes, I was upset to see my gift so casually discarded, but perhaps I was being selfish. I gave the gift freely, and it was then my father's to do with as he pleased. I am sure it gave him pleasure to surprise Mr. Holley with the gift. And he chose *my* gift! It must have been a good one if he thought Mr. Holley would like it.

Perhaps Uncle Tony's motives were similar. He felt bad about not having anything for his father on Christmas, and he knew it was better to give than to receive.

To this day, I keep a bottle of Old Spice in my cabinet as a reminder of those times. A little splash reminds me of a childhood filled with memories of a loving family, a father whose generosity was often anonymous (Just where did Santa get all those toys on Christmas?), and the lesson that we should give our gifts unselfishly.

Reflecting on the Story

Depending on the number of participants, you may want to create small groups to discuss these questions. Be sure to provide adequate discussion time before bringing the participants back into a large-group setting for overall feedback and response. Another option would be to provide the participants with journals and invite them to write their responses.

- What is the greatest gift you have ever given to someone? What made that gift so special, and why did you choose it?
- What is the greatest gift you have ever received? Describe how you felt when you received that gift and why it was so special.
- Reflect on your answers to the previous questions. Did you list material possessions? If so, now consider gifts that are nonmaterial — time, friendship, assistance, and so on. Re-examine the previous questions in light of those nonmaterial gifts.
- Recall a time you received a gift you did not really want. What was your reaction?
- Reflect on a time when your parents made a decision that you did not like but later came to understand. What made you change your mind? How did you feel toward your parents after you reached the new understanding?
- Reflect on the gifts God has given you. How do you use those gifts? What gifts or talents do you have that you are not using as you should? How can you use those talents more wisely?

Breaking Open the Message of the Story

Preparation

The following activities will assist the participants in breaking open the message of the story. Choose activities that are most appropriate for the group gathered and the time allotted.

Gather these items:

- ○ small slips of paper, one for each participant
- ○ pens or pencils, one for each participant
- ○ sale ads, catalogs, magazines, a few for each participant
- ○ scissors, one pair for each participant

○ drawing paper, one sheet for each participant

○ markers, colored pencils, or crayons, enough for each participant

○ copies of *The Catholic Youth Bible*™ or another Bible, one for each small group

The Perfect Gift

Provide each participant with a small slip of paper and a pen or pencil. Invite each person to write his or her name on the paper, fold it in half, and place it in the center of the room. Then invite each participant to select a slip of paper from the pile, read the name on it, and keep the name a secret. Provide each participant with a few sale ads, catalogs, magazines, and a pair of scissors. Ask each person to find the perfect gift for the person whose name he or she has chosen and cut it out of the ad, catalog, or magazine. Allow 10 minutes for the participants to complete this task. Go around the room and have each person present the gift he or she chose and the meaning behind it to the person whose name he or she drew from the pile. When everyone has done that, tell the participants they must now give their new gifts away to people who are not in the room. Have them explain who they chose and why. Conclude by inviting some general discussion about the activity and the need to be generous toward others.

The Greatest Gift

Distribute a sheet of drawing paper and some markers, colored pencils, or crayons to each participant. Invite the participants to draw a picture that represents the greatest gift they ever gave someone. Allow 5 minutes for this. Then ask the participants to share their drawings with the group. When they are done sharing, ask them to turn their papers over and draw something that represents the greatest gift they have ever received. This time, however, the gift cannot be a material possession. Allow 5 minutes for drawing and then follow with a discussion.

The Meaning of Talents

Divide the large group into small groups of seven or eight and provide each group with a Bible. Ask the small groups to read "The Parable of the Talents" from Matthew 25:14–30. Explain that in biblical times, *talent* referred to a sum of money. Have each group then prepare a short skit illustrating this parable in a modern setting. Give the groups 10 minutes to prepare. After the skits are presented, discuss how the groups represented talents. Did any groups use non-material gifts to represent talents? Remind the participants that God has given them physical abilities, gifts, and talents in order to serve us well in our lives.

Living the Story

Offer the following ideas to the participants as a way to continue the message of the story beyond the gathering. You might do this by listing all the ideas on a handout and sending it home, choosing one or two ideas to share and discuss with the participants, or listing the ideas on newsprint for review or discussion.

- Buy a simple, inexpensive gift for one of your parents. Wrap it nicely and present it as a surprise, just to say thank you.
- Find items in your bedroom that you no longer need. Donate the items to an agency or shelter that can use them.
- Volunteer your time. Examine your talents and find a way to share them with others. Be a tutor. Teach someone to dance. Play basketball with a child. Use your musical talent at a nursing home.
- Resolve to be grateful for all the gifts you receive during a regular day. Remember to say thank you for the kindnesses you experience each day.

Praying the Story

Preparation

Gather these items for the following prayer experience:

- a table
- a sheet of newsprint
- several bottles of glue
- candles and matches
- any other items that will enhance the prayer space
- construction paper of various colors, one sheet for each participant
- scissors, one pair for each participant
- pens or markers, one for each participant
- a Copy of *The Catholic Youth Bible*™ or another Bible

Process

1. Put the table in the center of the room, and place the newsprint and bottles of glue in the middle of it. Surround the newsprint with candles and other items you may have brought to enhance the prayer space. Provide each participant with a sheet of construction paper, a pair of scissors, and a pen or marker.

2. Proclaim 1 Corinthians 12:4–13,27–31. Then invite each participant to cut out a unique shape from the paper and to list on that shape three or four talents that he or she possesses.

3. Explain that the gifts and talents God gives us are meant to be used and given away. In the story, giving away a gift was deemed a bad thing by the young person. But in life, everything we have is a gift from God. God asks that we share these gifts and talents with others to make the world a better place.

4. Now ask the participants to approach the prayer table one by one and glue their lists of talents on the newsprint.

5. When all the participants have attached their lists to the newsprint, note the variety of shapes, colors, and talents that make up the collage. Then offer these comments in your own words:

> o Such is the body of Christ. We all contribute with our own talents in our own way. Each of us should be mindful of the call to share our gifts with others each and every day.

6. Ask the participants to gather around the table as you offer the following prayer:

> o Loving and gracious God, giver of all things,
>
> We thank you for all you have given us.
>
> We pray that you will bless us with kind hearts and loving souls.
>
> We pray that we will share what we have with our neighbors and that we will always use our talents to serve you.
>
> Keep us ever mindful of our own giftedness and talents and help us use them to make the world a better place.
>
> We thank you for giving us the gift of your son, Jesus, and we thank Jesus for sharing himself with us.
>
> We ask these things humbly in the name of your Son, Jesus Christ, our savior, our teacher, our gift.
>
> Amen.

Chapter 2

Feeding the Hunger

Key Themes

- Bread feeds the body and the soul.
- God will take care of our hunger and all our needs.
- Stories connect us to one another and to generations to come.

Scripture Connections

- Exodus 16:1–8 ("I am going to rain bread from heaven for you.")
- Deuteronomy 8:2–3,14–16 (Not by bread alone does one live.)
- Matthew 15:32–39 (Jesus feeds the four thousand.)
- John 6:22–35 ("I am the bread of life.")

The Story

To enrich the environment for this lesson, purchase a fresh loaf of bread (not sandwich bread) and place it in a basket in a prominent location in the gathering space.

Offer the following introduction before telling the story:

- In this story, the simple task of baking bread links generations of women in learning to understand and satisfy the hungers of the body and the soul.

Most of what I understand about God I learned from my parents, and not just from what they told me. I learned from watching how they lived day to day. Trusting God became natural to me because it was to them.

Many of our family traditions were God-centered but none more so than my mother's gift for baking bread. Both of my parents were children of Italian immigrants. My father's small family of five had a very comfortable life compared to the daily struggle of my mother's large family of fifteen. Her father and brothers were all miners who worked long, dangerous hours deep within the earth. It was left to the daughters to learn at an early age how to take care of the men. With a family of fifteen, it took every resource and talent they could muster to keep the household going. There was cooking, cleaning, tending the garden, all the daily chores required to take care of a family so large. My mother's family survived poverty with dignity by working together and especially by trusting God.

Mama loved to tell us the story of how she learned to bake bread at the age of eight. She told of climbing on a step stool to reach the high countertop where all the ingredients were laid out, and how it usually took two or three sisters to lift the 25-pound sack of flour. If you have ever made bread by hand, you know it is strenuous work to blend all the ingredients and then knead them into smooth, elastic dough. Mama always stressed how important it was to mark the dough with the sign of the cross after it was kneaded and covered to rest. The sign of the cross acted as a reminder that bread is a gift from God, and that it is in bread that God is revealed to us over and over. Bread was more than a need to fight off the hunger of hard times; it was a symbol of Mama's family's faithful trust in God, a symbol of their salvation.

When I was growing up, people always thought it was a treat to be at Mama's house on baking day. Her kitchen was like a bakery, warm and busy, with a slight film of flour covering the table and dusting the air. Friends loved having a piece of freshly baked bread right out of the oven and then taking a loaf home. Unfortunately, neither my sister nor I ever took the time to learn the art of bread making. We just reaped the benefits as if our mother would always be there to give us what we needed and wanted from her. But, sadly, that was not the case. When my mother died, my sister and I tried to keep up with all the traditions she had taught us. Unfortunately, baking bread was not one of them.

One day, several months after my mother passed away, my aunt Lillie was visiting with me. Aunt Lillie frequently spoke about the good old days, and she repeated the treasured stories of her childhood. Naturally, we got around to bread. She too loved to tell the story of learning to make it and how baking bread was a chore that the girls of the family did several times a week. I confessed to Aunt Lillie how disappointed I was in myself that I had never taken the time to learn how to make bread. I also shared that I felt as if I had let my mother down, believing that I had been groomed to take her place. That seemed more than a failure to me; it felt as if I had torn a page out of our family story. Thankfully, Aunt Lillie had the remedy. Although she was elderly, blind, and no longer had the strength to do the work, she suggested I pull the ingredients from my cupboards, and with her know-how and my sight and good hands, we could do it together. And we did. Aunt Lillie taught me how to feel the right texture of the dough and to mark it with the sign of the cross before it was covered to rest. As we sat talking and waiting for the final rise, I finally felt we had both honored the traditions our mothers had passed to us. I knew I now had a place among the many generations of women in my family who had been a part of this tradition.

It was a perfect batch. Each loaf was golden and delicious. It is funny how good bread not only eases our gnawing hunger but also feeds our souls. We are taught that Jesus is the bread of life. How amazing that Jesus chose something as ordinary and simple as bread to reveal himself to us. Finally, I understand what that means. Just as my bread feeds the body, so the bread that is Jesus feeds our spirits and our souls.

Now I am a part of the old stories that I continue to pass on to my own family. My children have learned to make bread. When I made the invitation to them, they were eager to learn. We do it together now, mostly for family gatherings. As we sit at our table and break the bread we have made, I am reminded of the table Jesus invites us to, where the bread that is his Body is broken and shared with all.

Reflecting on the Story

Depending on the number of participants, you may want to create small groups to discuss these questions. Be sure to provide adequate discussion time before bringing the participants back into a large-group setting for overall feedback and response. Another option would be to provide the participants with journals and invite them to write their responses.

- "Bread is life." What does this sentence mean to you? What does it mean to your faith life?
- Have you ever gone without food for so long that you felt like you were starving? Share the feeling of hunger. Share the feeling of having your hunger fed.
- What does it mean to feed the body and the soul?
- What are your special family stories? Who tells you those stories?
- Where does God fit in the stories of your family? in the stories of your life?

Breaking Open the Message of the Story

Preparation

The following activities will assist the participants in breaking open the message of the story. Choose activities that are most appropriate for the group gathered and the time allotted.

Gather these items:

○ frozen or refrigerated bread dough, a knife, and a plate (all optional for "The Art of Bread Making" activity)

○ copies of the bread maker's recipe, one for each participant

Ingredients

Invite a bread maker to join the gathering to talk about the ingredients in bread and the purpose of each ingredient. Ask the bread maker to bring different types of bread for the participants to sample. Afterward, divide the group into several small groups. Ask the small groups to compare the ingredients in bread to a small community, such as their own family. How is each ingredient significant to the finished product? How is each family member significant to their families?

The Art of Bread Making

Invite a bread maker to demonstrate the art of bread making. If your meeting space allows, the bread maker can actually teach the participants to make bread. He or she can do this by bringing the ingredients as well as a batch of already-risen dough (so the participants can knead it and mark it with the sign of the cross). If a baker is not available, consider buying a package of frozen bread dough. It usually comes in five- or six-roll packages. Remove the rolls from the package and set each on a plate to thaw. After the dough is completely thawed, have the participants knead it down, roll it out, and prepare it for the oven according to the directions on the package. Another option is to use refrigerated bread dough, which can be found in the dairy case of a grocery store. Simply divide the dough into the number of loaves you wish to produce. End the activity by giving the participants a copy of the recipe and instructions to bake bread at home with their families.

Family Traditions

Invite the participants to think about their own special family traditions. In small groups, have the participants share those special family traditions with one another. Telling our stories is a way to find common ground with others. Encourage the participants to listen attentively, searching for the experiences of family they have in common.

Living the Story

Offer the following ideas to the participants as a way to continue the message of the story beyond the gathering. You might do this by listing all the ideas on a handout and sending it home, choosing one or two ideas to share and discuss with the participants, or listing the ideas on newsprint for review or discussion.

- As a family, make it a habit to offer a blessing before meals.
- Strive to be bread for the world with a voice of compassion and justice for those who are hungry.
- Serve at a local soup kitchen. Invite your friends or family to do this with you.
- Make bread together. Talk about the ingredients and their purposes. Bless the bread and share it at your family meal.
- Interview a grandparent or elderly relative and ask him or her to share family stories with you. Record your conversation. Let it become your mission to keep the family stories alive for the next generation.

Praying the Story

Preparation

Gather these items for the following prayer experience:

- ○ a table
- ○ a loaf of fresh-baked bread
- ○ a basket for the bread

Process

1. Place the loaf of bread in the basket and set it on the prayer table. Gather the participants around the table in a circle. Talk about the significance of a simple loaf of bread, using these or similar comments:

- Bread is nourishing and satisfying to feed the hunger of the body. Bread is the element that Jesus chose as a means to offer himself to us over and over again.

Be sure the participants understand that they are not receiving the Eucharist, or Communion. That can happen only when a person receives consecrated bread and wine during the liturgy. In this prayer service, breaking bread with one another is a symbol of Jesus's call to each of us be the Body of Christ and to build the Reign of God.

2. Remove the loaf of bread from the basket, and break off a small piece. Then pass the bread around the circle and invite the participants to do the same.

3. Use the following blessing or one of your own choosing:

- Lord, Jesus, you reveal yourself to us in the breaking of the bread.
  At the Last Supper, you commissioned your friends
      to take and eat the bread that was your body.
  We ask that you bless this bread we share tonight,
      that it may strengthen us to share that commission to be
      your hands and heart in our world.
  Lord, as we eat this bread, we recommit to be your storytellers
      and to invite others to break bread with us at your table.
  Amen.

4. Invite the participants to eat their bread, and then offer one another a sign of Christ's peace to end the activity.

Chapter 3

Thanksgiving Touchdowns

Key Themes

- It feels good to be chosen.
- We enjoy the confidence that success gives us.
- Role models are important to us in learning how we should live our lives.
- God has chosen each of us.

Scripture Connections

- 1 Samuel 16:1–13 (David is anointed king.)
- Jeremiah 1:4–5 (God knew you before you were born.)
- Matthew 4:18–22 (Jesus chooses Peter and Andrew.)
- Matthew 12:15–21 (Jesus is God's chosen servant.)

The Story

Offer the following introduction before telling the story:

- We all go through many types of rejection in life: not making the team,
  not getting the part in a school play, not winning the award, not getting
  the date. It would be easy to remember only our defeats. Yet we also
  experience moments when we feel appreciated, accepted, successful,
  valued. In this story, a game of touch football changes the way a young
  boy finds acceptance in a most unlikely moment.

Thanksgiving Day always meant a visit to my grandfather's house, where the
whole family gathered. The day's events included a huge meal followed by a
touch football game. My father, being the oldest brother, captained one team,
and my uncle Ernest, the next oldest, captained the other. Sides were chosen
with victory in mind. Sure, this was a fun game, but in true family tradition,

there was no fun in losing.

I was the smallest, which meant I was always the last to be picked, and Uncle Ernie was the one who picked me. I was happy to be on his team because the other team might get mad at me if I messed up. I knew Uncle Ernie was happy to have me on his side.

And so the game began. I went out for a pass. I was open, and I caught the ball. Maybe it was due to my great speed and elusiveness that I was open on almost every play. Maybe it was because I was the little guy and wasn't considered a threat.

On one pass play, Uncle Ernie spotted me in the end zone (just short of the row of bushes), and I watched as he hurled the ball in my direction. I reached out, grabbed the ball, cradled it in my arms, and hung on for a touchdown! Perhaps it was luck, perhaps not. Later, once again, Uncle Ernie found his new favorite receiver for a second touchdown. Man, this was fun! Usually all the big kids got all the passes. Today was really my day!

I must confess that family members still dispute the number of touchdowns the rookie receiver caught that day. It was at least three, maybe even four. Over the years, Uncle Ernie and I have somehow raised the number to six or eight. Regardless, I was a hero for a day.

The last touchdown was the most spectacular, and I can still remember it vividly. Again, I was open in front of the bushes. This time Uncle Ernie's pass was a little high. I reached up as far as I could and snagged the ball while falling backward into the bushes. I held on! It was my fourth touchdown of the day.

Uncle Ernie came and grabbed me up in his arms and ran around the yard holding me high. We passed by the dining room window where my mother was watching, her face beaming with a smile. Uncle Ernie held up four fingers. "He scored four touchdowns!" he shouted.

I admit it wasn't the Super Bowl. (The Super Bowl hadn't even been invented then). It was not high school football or even a real team, but it was important.

I cannot recall the final score that day. (Surely our team won with that incredible performance!) I do recall feeling like a winner. Just holding on to the ball was victory enough.

Uncle Ernie showed confidence in me. I am sure I probably dropped the ball a few times that day, but he had the confidence to keep throwing to me. He trusted me. It was nice to be trusted, for someone to have confidence in me. Most important, Uncle Ernie picked me. How nice it was to be chosen. Someone chose me. That felt great!

On this day filled with Thanksgiving touchdowns, I was thankful to be chosen. Maybe it was not God who did the picking that day, but Uncle Ernie rated a close second, that was for sure.

Years later, I would return the favor, choosing Uncle Ernie to be my Confirmation sponsor. We were told to pick an adult who was a Christian role model for us, someone we wanted to be like. Maybe it was Uncle Ernie's sense of humor. Maybe it was his love for kids. Most likely, it was because he had taken a chance on a little guy that nobody wanted and turned him into a Thanksgiving hero.

Reflecting on the Story

Depending on the number of participants, you may want to create small groups to discuss these questions. Be sure to provide adequate discussion time before bringing the participants back into a large-group setting for overall feedback and response. Another option would be to provide the participants with journals and invite them to write their responses.

- Share about a time when you have felt the acceptance and love of God in your life.
- What is the greatest success you have ever experienced?
  Discuss the feeling you had at the time.
- Read Matthew 4:18–22. Reflect on how Peter and Andrew felt to be chosen by Jesus.
- If you have a favorite uncle or aunt or other role model, discuss the reasons he or she is special to you. What characteristics stand out about your relationship with that person?

Breaking Open the Message of the Story

Preparation

The following activities will assist the participants in breaking open the message of the story. Choose activities that are most appropriate for the group gathered and the time allotted.

Gather these items:

- O index cards, one for each participant
- O copies of *The Catholic Youth Bible*™ or another Bible, one for each

    participant
○   sheets of paper, two for each participant plus a couple extras
○   pens or pencils, one for each participant

Word Search

Using index cards, write a random name (other than those of the participants) on each card. You will need one card for each participant. On a sheet of paper, list the names in two columns in random order. Provide each participant with one index card. Then ask for two volunteers to serve as leaders. Provide the leaders with the list you created. The leaders choose teams in the order of the names you have noted on the list. As names are called out by the team leaders, tell the participants to join their assigned team accordingly. Once the teams have been named, ask them to find a spot in the meeting space to gather.

Distribute the bibles, telling the participants that the first team to find a passage with the word you call out will win that round. You may choose your own words or use the following:

- chosen
- call
- kindness
- love
- praise
- pride
- strength
- success
- trust

After a few rounds, declare a winner and then conduct a group discussion focusing on the ideas of being chosen earlier or later in the process, winning versus losing, and so forth.

Role Models

Distribute a blank sheet of paper and a pen or pencil to each participant. Ask the participants to think of role models in their life or in public life. Discuss the fact that all so-called role models or heroes are not necessarily positive role models. Have the participants each write down the name of a person who is a positive role model and then list the traits and attributes that make that person a good role model. Then ask them to turn their sheet of paper over and on the back write the name of a public figure who is possibly idolized and who could be a role model for some, but who is clearly not a positive role model. Then have the participants write the reasons why this person should not be considered a positive role model. When everyone is done, have them take turns explaining why they chose the role models they did.

Defeats and Successes

Distribute the paper and the pens or pencils. Ask the participants to divide their sheets into two columns and title the left column "Personal Successes" and the right column "My Defeats." Ask them to think of their own life experiences and list times when they have been "winners" and times when they have not. Allow 5 to 10 minutes for this. Ask each participant to share an example from his or her list. Some participants may choose not to share, which is fine. Then ask the participants to reflect on this question: Did any defeats lead to a success at a later time? Discuss how defeats and rejections in life serve as learning experiences and can sometimes lead to success later.

Living the Story

Offer the following ideas to the participants as a way to continue the message of the story beyond the gathering. You might do this by listing all the ideas on a handout and sending it home, choosing one or two ideas to share and discuss with the participants, or listing the ideas on newsprint for review or discussion.

- Identify someone in your life who has shown confidence in you and has taken a chance on you. Resolve to thank him or her in some small way in the upcoming week.
- Choose someone to compliment or lend a hand to. Teach a younger person something or just let him or her hang out with you for a little while. Be careful not to reject the young person later.
- Thank God. As you pray, thank God for choosing you. Thank God for choosing your family and friends.
- Learn about God. Search the Bible randomly for a word or theme. Find instances of Jesus's choosing his followers.

Praying the Story

Preparation

Have *The Catholic Youth Bible*™ or other Bible on hand for proclaiming the Scripture passage.

Process

1. Invite the participants to sit on the floor in front of you. Then offer the following prayer or one of your own choosing:

> ○ O loving and gracious God, as we gather today,
>
> We ask that you open our hearts so that we may truly be grateful to the many blessings we have.
>
> We ask this in the name of your Son, our Lord, Jesus Christ.
>
> Amen.

2. Invite a participant to proclaim Isaiah 42:1–6. Allow a few moments of silence afterward.

3. Now call the participants, by name, to stand with you. You will want to call them randomly but in groupings so that no one is standing alone, especially at the end.

4. Offer the following prayer:

> ○ My friends, just as I have called you today,
>   remember that God is calling you each day as well.
> You were chosen by a loving and caring God
>   to live a life of love, compassion, and kindness.
> May God bless you, keep you strong,
>   and always give you the courage and strength to follow the example of our Lord and Savior, Jesus Christ.
> We ask these things in the name of our good and gracious God.
> Amen.

Chapter 4

The Search

Key Themes

- We can learn from the poor decisions or mistakes we sometimes make.
- We can look to others for help along the way.
- God provides us with guidance and direction for all the choices we face.
- Life's journey is continuous. One ending is merely the beginning of another leg of the journey.

Scripture Connections

- Psalms 32:8 ("I will instruct you and teach you the way you should go.")
- Isaiah 30:19–21 (The Lord will guide you.)
- Matthew 7:13–14 (The right road is narrow.)
- 2 Corinthians 4:16–18 (Live by faith.)

The Story

Offer the following introduction before telling the story:

- Life is filled with choices. Some decisions are easy to make and we have no doubt what to choose. But every now and then, we struggle with our choice. Where do we turn for help? Often that help is right in front of us, but we just can't see it. In this story, a trip is filled with wrong turns, but in the end, the destination is finally reached with a little help along the way.

We were invited to join another church on its annual retreat, and together we chose the theme "In Search of . . . ," hoping to explore our search for faith, for love, for meaning in life. Our destination would be the Shady Grove Dude

Ranch, which is located in the northeastern part of Alabama, about two hours from our church. We started the trip with the other church's van leading the way. I took the last spot in the caravan, which consisted of six vehicles. It was a little past dark as we finally got on the interstate.

Most of the first part of our trip was filled with negotiations over who controlled the radio and what music we listened to. The other major discussion concerned how slow the van ahead of us was driving. It was foggy, so I assured everyone that was the reason for the slow pace of our caravan.

After a while, the van ahead of us exited for a restroom stop, and we followed. Only then were we surprised to discover that our caravan now consisted of just our two vehicles rather than the six we began with. The other driver explained that the first four vans had left us behind.

This bothered me a little, as I had never been to the Shady Grove Dude Ranch and was not sure exactly where it was. I pulled out the map that had been supplied to us and checked it out. It looked to be handwritten and obviously not to scale. It consisted of a bunch of intersecting, unlabeled lines with an occasional arrow or landmark along the way. I was sure where to exit the interstate and figured there would be signs to help us the rest of the way. So back into the two vans we piled and continued on.

I found the correct exit but immediately could see that our map was flawed. We came to a stop sign and had to turn left or right. But there was no stop sign on the map and, of course, no indication of which way we should turn. After a lively discussion with the designated navigator in the back seat, we took a left because the map had a little curve on it. And then we drove and drove and drove until we saw a sign up ahead. Finally, we had some help. Well, that was my thought until I read the sign: "Welcome to Georgia." Georgia?! I had no idea we were anywhere near the state of Georgia. I took the expected harassment from not only the passengers in my van but the passengers of the other van as well. "You should have turned right back there." I guess I had figured that out by then!

So we turned around and headed back to Alabama, continuing our search for the Shady Grove Dude Ranch. Sure enough, just a quarter mile or so past the interstate exit (to the right, naturally) was the highway we needed. It was clearly marked, so there was no mistaking we were on the correct road now. Of course we were still at the mercy of the curvy lines on the map, but there was one landmark to look for. A church would mark our next turn (to the right again). We proceeded cautiously, even though we were way past our scheduled arrival time. We drove and searched and drove and searched and drove and fussed and drove and searched.

You guessed it. No church. We finally decided it was time to turn around. We spotted a group of locals gathered in a parking lot and asked for help. Of course we were heading in the wrong direction, so once again we turned around, searching for our landmark. I am still not sure how, but after a short drive, a very large church appeared on our left. How had we missed it before? I have no idea, but there it was with a huge sign. This was definitely our turn.

The rest of the trip was slow and tedious as we crept down dark highways looking for tiny signs that led us to the Shady Grove Dude Ranch. Finally we arrived, expecting that everyone would be worried about us. Most of them had just arrived as well, though none had experienced quite the trip we had. Now it was time for the retreat to begin. For us, however, it had already begun, the trip there being a lesson in itself.

So often in life we set out for a destination — to live a good life, to be a success, to do the right thing. We get in a hurry or maybe we just don't pay attention. Often the signs that tell us the correct way are clearly in front of us, yet somehow we still miss them. So, instead of going "right," we take the wrong turn. If we are lucky, something happens in our life to get us straightened out and back on the right path. (Welcome to Georgia!)

How true this is of so many of us. Life becomes hectic, and we are so intent on living it — making the team, passing the exam, going to college, getting the promotion, getting married, raising a family, living the good life — that we lose our way. We might even drive right by the church, as I did, and not even notice. But when we do turn around, the church is there waiting, eager to be noticed. God, too, is always there for us, just waiting for us to pay attention. And when we do, we may be able to decipher what direction to turn on a dark and abandoned road. And what a wonderful feeling that is!

But making one right turn does not complete the journey. The search always continues. Along the way, we must be aware of the signs that guide us, ever conscious of our final destination. It helps to know that we all make some wrong turns along the way. But there is still hope — a friend to point the way, a sign along the road, a church, a loving and forgiving God — to get us back on the right track.

The weekend retreat ended on Sunday, and the trip home was a breeze. But life is more than one weekend. Soon we would all set out on other trips, hopefully a bit better prepared, but still searching.

Reflecting on the Story

Depending on the number of participants, you may want to create small groups to discuss these questions. Be sure to provide adequate discussion time before bringing the participants back into a large-group setting for overall feedback and response. Another option would be to provide the participants with journals and invite them to write their responses.

- Reflect on your own spiritual journey. Where did you first hear about God? Think of the people who have helped guide you along the way.
- What challenges have you faced along your spiritual journey? Reflect on where those experiences left you and how you were changed.
- Where do you look for guidance? What role does your faith play in helping you with tough decisions? As you have matured, how has your decision making changed?
- Look to the future. What is your goal, spiritually? What decisions do you see ahead that could affect your spiritual journey? Who or what can you rely on for help?

Breaking Open the Message of the Story

Preparation

The following activities will assist the participants in breaking open the message of the story. Choose activities that are most appropriate for the group gathered and the time allotted.

Gather these items:

- ○ sheets of blank paper, one for each participant
- ○ markers, one for each participant
- ○ a copy of *The Catholic Youth Bible*™ or another Bible

Spiritual Journey

Distribute the paper and the markers. Ask the participants to turn the paper the long way and write "My Spiritual Journey" at the top. Tell them to write their date of birth on the left side of the page and today's date on the right. Invite the participants to draw a timeline that depicts their spiritual journey to date. Request that they show significant life events that have shaped them, including spiritual events (Baptism, Bible school, and Communion), challenges (loss of loved ones, family problems), and critical decisions (both good and bad). Note that they can use code words or initials on their timelines for events that are private. Allow 10 to 15 minutes for this task, and then divide the large group into smaller groups of four to five to share some of the events they have listed.

Facing Challenges

Using the timeline the participants created in the "Spiritual Journey" activity, ask them to turn their papers over and again label the top "My Spiritual Journey." Have them divide the paper into two columns, writing "Today" on the left side and "The Future" on the right. Now ask them to list in each column challenges they are facing now and will face in the future. These could include keeping their grades up, getting into college, deciding what to study, and so forth. When they have completed this task, ask them to list in each column, next to each challenge, a source of strength and guidance they might use during these times (family members, school counselors, friends, the Scriptures, and so on.) Allow 5 to 10 minutes for the participants to complete these tasks. Then ask for volunteers to share their thoughts with the group.

Being Attentive to God

Ask the participants to stand at one end of the gathering space (perhaps at the back of the room) while you stand at the opposite location (the front of the room). Tell them you will be reading a Scripture verse and they are to listen as attentively as possible. They are not to speak or ask any questions while you conduct the reading. Open your Bible to Isaiah 30:19–21 and begin reading the passage as quietly as you possibly can. The goal is to read so quietly that the participants will not be able to hear you. When you finish, ask the participants to tell you what the reading was about. When they are unable to tell you, pose these questions: What are some of the things that make us unaware of the Word of God? Are there times when we hear or recognize God's Word or God's voice but aren't really being attentive?

Now ask the participants to find a place within the meeting room where they can sit quietly. Ask them to spend 5 to 10 minutes reflecting on this question: What do I need to do to be more attentive to God's voice, guidance, or direction in my life?

(This activity is adapted from Mary Ann Hakowski, *Sharing the Sunday Scriptures with Youth: Cycle A*, pp. 109–110.)

Living the Story

Offer the following ideas to the participants as a way to continue the message of the story beyond the gathering. You might do this by listing all the ideas on a handout and sending it home, choosing one or two ideas to share and discuss with the participants, or listing the ideas on newsprint for review or discussion.

- Keep a journal. Once a week, record in your journal the answers to the following questions: What moment over the past week did I feel closest to God? When did I feel farthest away? What did I do this week to keep my spiritual life on track?
- Show someone the way. If you know someone who needs help, offer to lend a hand.
- Work to improve. If you have a particular weakness or bad habit, vow to stop for one day, then one week. Substitute the destructive behavior with something positive.
- Plan ahead. Look for opportunities to strengthen your personal spirituality.
- Read the story of a saint or an early Church leader.

Praying the Story

Preparation

Gather these items for the following prayer experience:

- a table
- a candle and matches
- a copy of *The Catholic Youth Bible*™ or another Bible

This session will conclude with a reading of the story of the walk to Emmaus from the Gospel of Luke. Have a volunteer prepare the reading ahead of time so he or she can proclaim it powerfully and reverently.

Process

1. Prepare a prayer space in the center of the room. On the prayer table,

place a candle, matches, and a Bible. Invite the participants to join you in the prayer space as you light the candle. Open with the following words or words of your own choosing:

> ○ Loving and gracious God,
> We invite you today to send your Holy Spirit to us as teacher, guide, and inspiration.
> We pray that we always remain open to your Word,
> aware of the many signs you give us to guide us along the way.
> Amen.

2. Invite the volunteer reader to come forward and proclaim Luke 24:13–35. Allow a few moments of silence to follow.

3. Now ask for participants to share prayers of thanksgiving for times that God has been there to guide them, or prayers of petition for help with an upcoming decision or situation.

4. After everyone has had time to share, conclude with the following prayer:

> ○ O God,
> We beseech you to be with us this day.
> Keep us strong and always on the right path.
> We, like the two disciples in the Gospel, may not recognize your presence at times,
> but we pray that with courage and perseverance that we will come to know you, to love you, and to follow the path set by your Son,
> our savior, Jesus Christ.
> Bless us with your guidance in all we do.
> Look favorably on the prayers and petitions we have offered in the name of your Son, Jesus.
> Amen.

Chapter 5

Sight

Key Themes

- We need more than good eyes to see clearly.
- Faith does not require perfect eyesight.
- Sight alone does not give one true perspective.
- Family traditions are an important part of family life.

Scripture Connections

- Matthew 9:27–31 (Jesus restores the sight of two blind men.)
- Mark 10:46–52 (Bartimaeus is healed.)
- John 20:24–29 (Blessed are those who have not seen but believe.)

The Story

Offer the following introduction before telling the story:

o   Sight is a powerful sense that helps us identify and understand the world around us, but to truly "see," one must look with the eyes of faith.

In this story, a woman's lifelong journey through blindness reveals her clear and unwavering faith.

Aunt Lillie's eyes were milky and out of focus. When I was young and curious and had no tact, I would move around and watch her try to find me. When she could not look directly at me, I wanted to know why. I hurt her feelings because I didn't know at the time that it was the best she could do. I never really understood how bad her eyesight was, and that she was actually blind by medical standards. After all, my mother trusted her without question with my brothers, sister, and me. She was a second mother to us, doting on us as if we were her own. Before the era of the mall, we would spend many a Saturday together shopping downtown. We would take the bus to town. Aunt Lillie knew where everything was and how to get wherever we wanted to go. All she asked was that we hold her hand in the crowd and tell her the street names so she could get her bearings. We never wandered away from her, as we were too afraid of getting lost. She needed our sight but not more than we needed her "eyes" and her sharp senses to stay safe. We had absolute faith in Aunt Lillie's ability to look out for us. Long, exhausting afternoons we spent together, going from one department store to another before dragging ourselves home loaded down with packages that held something for everyone.

Aunt Lillie was born with a degenerative eye disease. As a school girl in the late 1920s, she never mastered reading or writing because she could not see well enough to distinguish the letters. Because of this, she was held back in fourth grade three times and was labeled "uneducable." Finally, my aunt had enough and dropped out of school. There was too much work to do at home for a girl who could not pass fourth grade. Things might have been different if her parents had understood how poor her eyesight actually was. Imagine if Aunt Lillie had been born in a different time, a time like the present, when every child is encouraged to achieve and succeed regardless of challenges.

When I think of Aunt Lillie, I try to imagine what my life would be like if my eyes were foggy and useless. I doubt I could be as brave and productive with my life as she was with hers. But Aunt Lillie never felt sorry for herself; she fervently believed that she could do whatever she set her mind to. She awoke everyday with a purpose, a routine, a goal, and a sense of gratitude to have a new day ahead of her. She slept every night the good sleep of a person whose day was well spent.

Aunt Lillie had a sixth sense. Later as an adult, I laid my newborn in Aunt Lillie's arms for the first time. She held my son close to her face and studied him, using each of her senses. She knew his smell, his feel, and the kiss of his sweet baby skin. My son was content and safe in her arms. That is how she knew all of us, friends and family — by the sound of our steps coming into a room, by the way we breathed, by our scents. She was that intimately aware of each of us.

The most remarkable thing about Aunt Lillie was her uncanny ability to believe with such clarity. Her faith was not only her hallmark but also the legacy she left to those of us who loved her. She relied on faith fiercely, defending it, preaching it, and living it. People were drawn to her because of her happy spirit, wanting a little of what she had. Aunt Lillie had a joyful faith, and it was her constant companion. That is what she shared with others.

Aunt Lillie has been gone for several years now. At her funeral, I offered her eulogy. I reminded those gathered that she had the clearest vision of anyone I had ever known. When anyone asked a question of faith, she had a clear, firm answer, and she never wavered in her judgment or her opinions. She spoke with confidence because hers was such an intimate relationship with God. If any of us needed strong prayers, we called Aunt Lillie. She believed more strongly and truly than anyone I have ever known. When we called her our prayer warrior, she would smile because she knew it was true!

Aunt Lillie's eyes may not have worked properly, but she had keen sight, seeing what most eyes cannot. By necessity, she skipped the facade and went straight to the heart of each of us, learning us from the inside out. Surely that is a lesson to remember. True sight. There is an image in ancient church art of the all-seeing eye of God. I imagine this eye as a kind of radar that scans humanity and sees all. I think of it like Aunt Lillie's eyes, always scanning the heart of humanity. Perhaps in heaven we will all see as she did.

Reflecting on the Story

Depending on the number of participants, you may want to create small groups to discuss these questions. Be sure to provide adequate discussion time before bringing the participants back into a large-group setting for overall feedback and response. Another option would be to provide the participants with journals and invite them to write their responses.

- Describe a time when you have felt blinded. Perhaps you were leterally blinded by the sun or a bright light and not able to see clearly. Or maybe you were blinded by circumstances or events that you did not expect. How did you feel in either situation to have your ability to see clearly temporarily disturbed?
- What does it mean to you to see with the eyes of faith?
- Think of someone you know who sees clearly, not only with his or her eyes but also with his or her mind and heart? How has this person been an example of faith to you?
- If you spent a day without sight, how do you think the experience would make you feel? Think of a few words to describe the feeling (alone, afraid, humble, humiliated, and so on).

Breaking Open the Message of the Story

Preparation

The following activities will assist the participants in breaking open the message of the story. Choose activities that are most appropriate for the group gathered and the time allotted.

Gather these items:

- O   a pair of dark sunglasses with lenses smeared with grease
- O   blindfolds, one for the "Altered Sight" activity and one for each participant for the "Lack of Sight" activity
- O   a pair of magnified reading glasses
- O   a pair of prescription glasses
- O   a pair of tinted swimming goggles
- O   a kaleidoscope
- O   an eye patch with a small hole poked in the middle
- O   a focus object, such as an oddly-shaped rock, a piece of wood, an unusual shell, an abstract piece of art, or a small sculpture
- O   sheets of blank paper, two for each participant
- O   pens, one for each participant
- O   a drawing of a geometric or simple design
- O   several sheets of newsprint
- O   several markers

Altered Sight

This perspective activity will give the participants an opportunity to see in a different way, without the clear use of their eyes. Place the sunglasses, blindfold, magnified reading glasses, prescription glasses, swimming goggles, kaleidoscope, and eye patches in different locations (perhaps on tables or chairs) throughout the room.

Divide the large group into seven small groups, and assign each group one of the locations you have designated. When the participants reach their assigned locations, ask them to turn their backs to you (in other words, they need to not be facing you). Explain that they will all be asked to focus on the object you are going to place in the center of the room. Each small-group member will take a quick turn viewing the object using the sight tool provided at their assigned location. During this sneak peek, each person should make note of any particular characteristics of the object, such as shape, color, size, and any other defining details. While each group member does this, the other group members must keep their backs to the center of the room so they will not see the object before viewing it with their group's sight tool. Continue this process until all group members have seen the object.

Gather the participants back into the large group, distribute paper and pens, and instruct the participants to write a description of the object as they saw it. Give them time to read their responses aloud to see how they compare. Ask the participants to describe their experience of altered sight. Was it a struggle? Were they able to use other senses to compensate?

Lack of Sight

Before the gathering, choose a simple design or simple geometric pattern to describe to the group (for example, the Olympic logo of interlocking rings or a coat of arms). Keep the design or pattern hidden from the group. Give each participant a sheet of paper and a pen. Then blindfold each participant (or simply ask them to close their eyes). Instruct them to listen to you carefully, noting that you will describe a design to them that they must draw (while blindfolded), using only your descriptive words as their guide.

Speak slowly and clearly, giving simple descriptions and directions. Do not allow the participants to speak or ask questions while you are describing the design. Repeat the instructions a second time if needed, but no more than that.

When you have finished and have given the participants ample time to complete their drawings, ask them to remove their blindfolds and look at their drawings. Show them the original design you were describing. Allow them time to look at one another's drawings.

Conclude by leading a large-group discussion of the following questions:
• How were you impaired and frustrated in trying to accomplish the task?
• Did you listen more intently to the instructions because you could not see?
• Could you picture the design in your mind?
• Describe how you did or did not feel limited by your lack of sight.

Attitude Anagram

Divide the large group into several small groups. Give each group a sheet of newsprint and a marker. Explain that the story they have heard is about a woman's attitude and her choice to rely on the talents she had rather than dwell on what she lacked. Perspective is determined by attitude. Instruct the small groups to create an anagram of the words ATTITUDE and PERSPECTIVE. Tell them to begin by writing each word vertically down the left side of their sheets of newsprint. Then instruct them to choose words for each letter, that describe their understanding of a positive attitude and a clear and healthy perspective. Give the groups time to share their anagrams in the large group.

Living the Story

Offer the following ideas to the participants as a way to continue the message of the story beyond the gathering. You might do this by listing all the ideas on a handout and sending it home, choosing one or two ideas to share and discuss with the participants, or listing the ideas on newsprint for review or discussion.

- Practice seeing with the eyes of faith. Remember, faith is believing in what you cannot see.
- Begin to look at people from the inside out. You may find that as you get to know someone, and the more you begin to like him or her, the better he or she will look! It is true that beauty is only skin deep.
- Pay attention to your own attitude. Does it need a little fine tuning to become more positive and productive?
- Notice people who are labeled as disabled. Think of what you can learn from their determination to live successful lives.
- Challenge yourself to focus on what you can do rather than on what you cannot do.

Praying the Story

Preparation

Gather the group in a circle. Explain that the closing prayer will be a blessing of the senses and that the leader will speak the blessing and instructions.

Process

Read the blessing and instructions. (The instructions are enclosed in parentheses.)

○ Creator God,

We gather to thank you for the gifts of sight, hearing, touch, taste, and smell, which we use to fully participate in your glorious creation.

We ask your blessing upon us.

(Cover eyes with hands.)

Lord, bless our eyes, that we may see with the true vision of faith.

(Cover ears with hands.)

Lord, bless our ears, that we may hear you in the voices of our neighbors and the sounds of your creation.

(Raise hands, palms up.)

Lord, bless our hands, that they may be a source of comfort and care to others.

(Cover mouth with hands.)

Lord, bless our mouths, that we may taste and be nourished by the bounty of the earth.

(Cover nose with hands.)

Lord, bless our noses, that we may breathe the sweet air that fills our lungs and gives us life.

Good and gracious God,

You are our divine parent who has made us whole and complete in your love.

May we bless others as you bless us.

We pray this in the name of your Son, Jesus Christ, our Lord.

Amen.

Chapter 6

Hanging Out on the Fringe

Key Themes

- "Comfort zones" are less comfortable than they are binding.
- Diversity is a gift we can bring to relationships.
- Relationships may not last a lifetime, but they serve an important function.

Scripture Connections

- Proverbs 3:29–30 (Do not harm your friend who trusts you.)
- Matthew 5:43–48 (Love your neighbor, but also love your enemy.)
- Luke 14:7–11 (People who exalt themselves will be humbled; people who humble themselves will be exalted.)

The Story

Offer the following introduction before telling the story:

- High school is fertile ground for learning life lessons that teach us to be open and welcoming to people who are different from us. This story describes a lesson that taught two unsuspecting students how to step beyond their perceived roles to become good friends.

I was not the most popular girl in school, but I was so comfortably entrenched in the society of school that I could maneuver in and out of different groups with ease. I was included in everything. I had people to hang out with on the weekends and a date to all the big events. I had friends and boyfriends. I was mainstream.

My senior year began on a high note. I can't describe how it felt to walk the hallowed halls as a member of the reigning senior class. Most of us had senioritis from the first day of school that year, which meant we were less interested in academics than we were in maintaining a social high and making memories. That is how I started twelfth grade.

Our school was an old, three-story dinosaur with three stairwells, no elevators, and only three minutes between classes. We had to hustle to get where we needed to be, especially if a locker stop was necessary. The school was not air conditioned, so in late summer, when school began, a three-minute run up and down the stairs could work up a mini-heatstroke. Trust me, any opportunity to avoid the mad rush was desirable, and I hit the mother lode one steamy day in early September.

I had gone to school with Mary Ann for eight years, but during high school we rarely, if ever, spoke to each other. Don't get me wrong; I was always nice to her, but nice in that vacant, generic way, with a plastic smile. She was "fringe," after all, and pretty happy to be there. Everything about her screamed fringe. For example, most of us went to great lengths to make our hideous school uniforms appear somewhat stylish, which meant we broke nearly every dress code rule. Mary Ann, however, was the poster child for the perfect uniform. She wore the blazer, the knee socks, and the black tie shoes. Even worse, she carried a briefcase! It was the ultimate status breaker of the class of 1972. She looked more like a teacher than a student. At times I felt embarrassed for her. She was just so out of touch (or so I thought). But I'll give her this: she was the queen of academia. She was intelligent, directed, and diligent.

One day in September, Mary Ann showed up at school on crutches. It was treacherous to climb three flights of stairs among hundreds of students rushing to get to their first-period class. Mary Ann and I had our first-period class together. We sat near each other, and, out of curiosity, I asked her what had happened. She described the freak fall that had resulted in her fractured ankle. She was worried about maneuvering from class to class, even with permission from the office to leave her classes a few minutes early. My devious little mind was spinning. I could help Mary Ann and at the same time escape the dull drone of my own classes simply by offering to help her carry her books! After all, this was a Catholic high school, where service was always encouraged. So we arranged it. I had permission to help Mary Ann for at least two weeks. Every day I would meet her at her class 10 minutes before the end of the period to carry her books. She would make her way slowly and painfully down hallways and up the stairs. In those first few days, this was a very long and awkward 10 minutes. We had so little in common that any conversation was hard work. Still, we tried to find things to talk about to fill the uncomfortably silent minutes, and each day it got easier.

One morning I discovered, to my surprise and shock, that Mary Ann had a personality—a good personality! She was funny and interesting, and she had such amazing self-confidence. She really liked herself. Mary Ann was the type of person I admired—a person who was comfortable in her own skin and didn't care what others thought about her. The more we talked, the more we discovered what we had in common. It was incredible! The old saying "You shouldn't judge a book by its cover" is true! I was guilty of making that judgment, but that goes both ways. Mary Ann had thought of me as a socializing airhead incapable of producing one profound thought. I couldn't believe how easy it was to bridge the gap between cool and uncool. All it took was time, interest, and willingness to admit that labels are destructive barriers that block people from one another.

Mary Ann and I began to spend time together outside of school. We lived in the same neighborhood, so we would get together after school and on Saturdays. As we became friends, we began inviting our other friends to join us. I cannot speak for Mary Ann, but for me a whole new world opened up. I had always felt smug about being cool, but the truth was that I was narrow and limited, and nothing was cool about that. I had done what I hated most: I had built a wall around my cushy life. I rarely stepped beyond it and kept all the "wrong" people out. Becoming friends with Mary Ann was like tearing down a wall and seeing how huge the world really was.

Mary Ann and I began a relationship that would see us through difficult times and happy ones, boyfriends and breakups, parent troubles and college worries, weddings, divorce, and even death. Eventually, she moved away, and over time we lost touch. Even now I pull out old letters she wrote to me throughout the years. I am never sad that we're not still in touch because I realize all friendships are not meant to last a lifetime, but they do last as long as they are needed. We may be no more than a moment in someone's life, but that moment can be life changing.

Reflecting on the Story

Depending on the number of participants, you may want to create small groups to discuss these questions. Be sure to provide adequate discussion time before bringing the participants back into a large-group setting for overall feedback and response. Another option would be to provide the participants with journals and invite them to write their responses.

- Think about two or three of your closest friends. What do you have in common with them? Discuss or write down the main characteristics of those friends.

- Describe a time when you sought a new relationship in order to add a new or different dimension to your life. Did that new relationship threaten an existing relationship? How did you solve the problem?
- Have you ever reached out to someone you perceived as "different" from you? How did you do it? What were the results?

Breaking Open the Message of the Story

Preparation

The following activities will assist the participants in breaking open the message of the story. Choose activities that are most appropriate for the group gathered and the time allotted.

Gather these items:

- ○ sheets of paper, two for each participant
- ○ pens or pencils, one for each participant
- ○ index cards, one for each participant

Friendship Quotations

Spend a few minutes discussing the following quotations about friendship taken from the book *She Said . . . He Said: Teens Speak Out on Life and Faith*:

> Friends are those people with whom we have detailed conversations. Even if they do not answer back, we know they are listening. (P. 9)

> A great friend is like a favorite movie that you watch over and over and never get tired of. Every time you watch it, you find out something different and new. (P. 22)

> True friends are the people who ask you how you are and wait for an answer. (P. 22)

Distribute the paper and pens or pencils and ask the participants to write their own friendship quotations. Allow a few minutes for them to do this. Then ask for a few volunteers to share their quotes, or divide the large group into smaller groups for sharing.

Guess Who?

Provide the participants each with an index card and a pen or pencil. Then invite them to write a brief, positive paragraph about themselves, ending with the question, "Who am I?" Note that they will be sharing these cards with one another. After a few minutes, collect the cards and read them one by one, giving the group the opportunity to guess who's who.

Written Affirmation

Give each participant a sheet of paper and a pen or pencil. Instruct the participants to write their names on their papers and pass them to the person at their left. Each person then writes a positive comment about the person whose name is on the paper. When everyone has written a comment for all the participants in the group, return each paper to its owner. Allow the participants a few moments to read what everyone wrote about them. (*Note:* This activity works best for a group of participants who know one another well.)

Living the Story

Offer the following ideas to the participants as a way to continue the message of the story beyond the gathering. You might do this by listing all the ideas on a handout and sending it home, choosing one or two ideas to share and discuss with the participants, or listing the ideas on newsprint for review or discussion.

- Challenge yourself to make a new friend who is different from you and your core group of friends.
- There are always people who seem to be alone even in the midst of a crowd—between classes, in the cafeteria, at a pep rally. Speak to those people. Start by saying a simple hello. Ask if you might sit with them during lunch. Smile at them when you pass in the hallway.
- Pray each day to be open to the surprise gift of a new friend. Pray for wisdom and clear vision to recognize God in the faces of all your classmates.

Praying the Story

Preparation

Gather these items for the following prayer experience:

○ a table

○ a candle and matches

○ a copy of *The Catholic Youth Bible*™ or another Bible

Process

1. Prepare a prayer table within the gathering space. Use a candle as a symbol of the ever-present light of Christ. Display a Bible prominently.

2. Invite the participants to stand in a circle around the prayer table. Light the candle, reminding the participants that the light of Christ is among them and within them.

3. Ask a participant to proclaim Luke 10:25–37. Allow a few moments of silence to follow.

4. Offer the following comments, which are adapted from *The Catholic Youth Bible*™ article "Discrimination in Jesus's Time" (near Luke 10:25–37):

○ In Jesus's day, the Samaritans were despised by Jews, even though Abraham was the father of faith for both groups.

○ Jesus's making a Samaritan the hero of the story would have given the lawyer and other people something to think about.

○ Imagine that this story takes place in your community. Who are the Samaritans, that is, people who are judged and rejected? How does this reflection affect your understanding of discrimination and stereotypes?

○ It seems that when we have a real relationship with others, even with those who are different from us, we are less likely to be prejudiced or to discriminate or stereotype others.

○ Each of us is called to work in our neighborhoods, schools, workplaces, and communities to invite all people to get to know one another better so that all "Samaritans" are regarded as good.

5. Invite the participants to think about someone they know (or have read or heard about) that has reached out to others. Invite the participants (one at a time) to say aloud the name of that individual, using the words "Lord, help us to be more like . . . (name of individual)."

6. When all who wish to speak have done so, conclude with the following prayer or one of your own choosing:

- Loving God,
  You appear to us in the faces of strangers,
      but we cannot find you there unless we learn to look for you.
  The story of the Good Samaritan shows us that our expectations of
      others can, at times, be wrong, and at those times we must be
      prepared to open our minds and hearts to change.
  Teach us to seek the treasure that lies within each person.
  We pray this in the name of your Son who loved and accepted
      all people.
  Amen.

Chapter 7

Mom Was Right

Key Themes

- Lessons we learn as children often stay with us for a lifetime.
- God places people in our midst to help us right our wrongs.
- God's love not only forgives but also forgets.

Scripture Connections

- Matthew 18:21–22 (We must forgive others many times.)
- Mark 12:28–31 (No other commandments are greater than the first two commandments.)
- Luke 15:31 (Repentance and forgiveness are cause for celebration.)

The Story

Offer the following introduction before telling the story:

- The most valuable and important lessons are those we learn in relationship with others, because that is where the golden rule begins to make sense: treat others as you want to be treated.

There was a time when I wished for a little switch to turn off my mother's voice, especially those times when I knew she was right! Embedded in my memory are so many of her sayings, especially this one: "Do good and forget it. Do bad and remember it." It was on the playground in the first grade that I remember vividly, and with shame, the day my mother's words came true.

Recess was the high point of the day. Like first graders do, we used our time running wild, playing games, chasing one another. On this particular day, the girls were all playing crack the whip, and I was the leader. We would run in zig-zags all over the playground, dragging the girls at the end, who were squealing with delight and exhaustion because they had to run so much faster.

It was a great game, and we were having so much fun until one of the girls in the whip, Rita, decided she wanted to be the leader. I said no because it was still my turn. Rita got mad and quit. Not only did she quit, but she began taking people from our game away with her. I had this great idea to take control of the situation and make Rita pay. And pay dearly she did. I got my gang of girls together, and wherever Rita was playing with new friends, we would go. I would convince her friends to come with my group, leaving her all alone. I could be very persuasive when I wanted to be. And so it went that whenever she would join a group, my ever-growing gang would swoop in and snatch those friends away, too, until I had every girl on the playground holding hands in a long line led by me. I'll admit that although I pranced around at the front of this line knowing I had won the battle, I did not feel great about it. I remember wishing the bell would ring to end recess, secretly hoping the bell would also end the feud. But no bell rang.

Finally, with no girls left to play with her, Rita broke down. I didn't feel satisfied for having won the battle and making Rita cry, especially when I saw her older sister. My gut reaction was fear! That seventh grader was going to crawl all over me! I looked around nervously for my own older sister, an eighth grader, but she was nowhere to be found. Rita and her sister, hand in hand, approached us, and as they did, my "gang" backed away from me. I was too afraid to move, although I like to think I looked bold standing there ready to face them. Rita's sister bent down and put her arms around us, pulling both of us close to her. I couldn't believe how kind she was, never once calling me mean or hateful (both of which I deserved). She just asked us if we could try to play together because it was sad when anyone was left out. She was right. Rita was crying, and I was miserable. We said we were sorry to each other and we really meant it. Hand in hand, we went back to playing. I am convinced divine intervention made recess go on so long that day in order to give us every opportunity to make a right out of a wrong.

There's nothing earth-shattering about children at play, in a fight, then at play again. Children have this amazing ability to put things behind them and go on. It is the ultimate letting go. Rita and I never spoke of it. When it was over, it really was over.

Telling this story now brings both shame and joy to me. If God does indeed cry, I knew I was the cause of any tears shed that day. We are taught that sin is communal. What we do breaks the harmony and peace of our relationships with one another and, worse, puts distance between us and God. But it is not God backing away from us, rather it is us ashamed and disgraced by our actions. I saw God so clearly that day in the actions of a seventh-grade girl who, wisely and kindly, led two friends back together.

My mother was right. I have remembered this all my life. This one little incident has done more to shape the person I am than any other in my life. Being forgiven is the most perfect gift anyone can give another person. Now I am careful, very careful, to respect and honor other people and to always seek God in them. And when necessary, I try with all my heart to forgive.

I hate to admit it, but Mom was right.

Reflecting on the Story

Depending on the number of participants, you may want to create small groups to discuss these questions. Be sure to provide adequate discussion time before bringing the participants back into a large-group setting for overall feedback and response. Another option would be to provide the participants with journals and invite them to write their responses.

- Discuss a time when your actions separated you from your friends or family. How did you repair the damage?
- "Forgiveness is a gift." What does this mean to you? Share a time when you have received or given this gift.
- Recall when a mediator was needed to help bring you back into a relationship that had been strained. What guidance did you rely on to bring you and that individual back together?
- Share about a time when you were pulled into the middle of a situation between friends. How did you help them achieve peace?
- Think of the people in your life who have modeled what a good and loving relationship looks like. What are the characteristics of that kind of relationship?

Breaking Open the Message of the Story

Preparation

The following activities will assist the participants in breaking open the message of the story. Choose activities that are most appropriate for the group gathered and the time allotted.

Gather these items:

- ○ sheets of paper, one for each participant
- ○ pen or pencils, one for each participant
- ○ small notebooks, one for each participant

Conflict Role-Play

Create a few situations of conflict that threaten relationships (for example, two friends trying out for the same position on a football team or the lead in a school play). Ask the participants to choose a partner with whom to role-play each situation. Then have them switch characters and role-play the other viewpoint. Give them an opportunity to discuss what it is like to view a situation from both sides.

Words of Wisdom

Our mothers can be very wise. Distribute the paper and the pens or pencils, and then invite the participants to create a list of their own mothers' or fathers' favorite words of wisdom that they would like to remember and pass on to their own children.

Memory Journal

Provide a notebook for each participant. Invite the participants to begin a personal memory journal. In it they should write the events and situations they witness daily that both damage and heal relationships. These can be situations they experience themselves or observations of other relationships. The object is to help them learn what works and what does not work in relationships. Give them several minutes to begin journaling their reflections from this gathering time.

Forgiveness Rituals

Many cultures and religious traditions include forgiveness rituals. For example, in Ecuador, on New Year's Eve many families make a scarecrow out of straw and pin a list of the misdeeds of everyone in the family on it. At midnight this list, or will, as it is called, is read aloud, and the scarecrow and the will are set on fire. As they burn, so do the family's faults, so that everyone begins the new year fresh and free. Jewish people think about the misdeeds of the past months during the New Year time from Rosh Hashanah to Yom Kippur. Some empty the lint or crumbs from their pockets into running water as a means of washing away the sins of the year. Divide the large group into small groups to discuss other types of forgiveness rituals the participants know about. You might also consider asking each group to create a simple ritual for future use.

Living the Story

Offer the following ideas to the participants as a way to continue the message of the story beyond the gathering. You might do this by listing all the ideas on a handout and sending it home, choosing one or two ideas to share and discuss with the participants, or listing the ideas on newsprint for review or discussion.

- Be a peacemaker. When situations arise that separate your friends from one another at school, try to help them solve the problem and forgive one another.
- The movie *Groundhog Day* (1993, 101 minutes, rated PG) is a good example of how we are given so many opportunities to "do it until we get it right." Suggest that the participants rent the movie and watch it with friends or family members. Just how many chances does God give us to "get it right"?
- WWJD? Consider what Jesus would do to prevent conflict and to end conflict.
- Ask for help. Learn to seek the wisdom and guidance of a trusted adult when a situation is beyond your control.
- Look for opportunities to model kindness, consideration, and patience.

Praying the Story

Process

1. Bring the participants together for prayer by inviting them to gather in a circle, facing away from the center. Then tell them that you are going to read a series of statements. If the statement applies to them, they are to take a step forward (moving away from the center of the circle). The object is to illustrate how their actions separate them from the community and from God.

2. Read each statement slowly, giving the participants a few seconds for reflection if needed. (You may add any other statements that have significance for the group assembled.)

- o   If you have ever spoken unkindly about a friend, take a step forward.
- o   If you have gossiped about someone, harming their reputation, take a step forward.
- o   If you have ever lied to someone close to you, take a step forward.
- o   If you have ever hurt someone with hateful words and cruel actions, take a step forward.
- o   If you have ever held a grudge, take a step forward.
- o   If you have ever refused to forgive when it was asked of you, take a step forward.

3. Now invite the participants to stay where they are and turn around to face the center of the circle and one another. It is important at this point that they pay attention to how separated they have become from one another. Point out that our sins isolate us from one another and from God.

4. Tell the group you are going to read another series of statements. Again, when the statement applies to them, they take a step forward, this time toward the center of the circle.

- o   If you have ever apologized to a friend even though you were not at fault, take a step forward.
- o   If you have ever tried to bring together friends who were fighting, take a step forward.
- o   If you have you ever asked God's forgiveness, take a step forward.
- o   If you have ever made friends with someone who had no friends, take a step forward.
- o   If you would rather live in peace than in anger, take a step forward.

5. By this time, the participants should be back in a close circle. Ask them to join hands and then offer the following prayer or one of your own:

    ○   Our good and loving God,

We ask you to look kindly on us when we struggle to live and love as you want us to.

Teach us to be generous in our words and deeds so that we may live together in friendship and peace.

When we separate ourselves from each other because of sin, it is your forgiveness that brings us close again and sets us free.

Let us never forget that it is your love we offer to one another.

It is your love that keeps us going.

Hear our prayer, O Lord, we pray.

Amen.

Chapter 8

The Stick

Key Themes

- God gives us others for support and guidance.
- We must live in a spirit of gratitude.
- We are never alone in our journey of life.

Scripture Connections

- Isaiah 40:28–31 (God strengthens those who are weak and tired.)
- Mark 6:7–13 (Take nothing with you but a walking stick.)
- John 14:19–20 (God will give you another helper.)

The Story

Before the participants gather, place a simple walking stick in a prominent location in the meeting space. Then offer the following introduction before telling the story:

> o Life's journey presents us with a variety of experiences. Moments of joy and happiness are often followed by times of sadness and disappointment. This story reminds us that we are not alone in our journey. God has placed friends and family at our side to support us, teach us, and guide us every step of the way.

Our group had planned a Sunday morning hike at a local state park in preparation for a journey to World Youth Day. We were expecting a 13-mile hike in Denver as part of the pilgrimage to the vigil site, so a little preparation was in order. Karen, our leader, promised this would be an easy hike—only 6 miles or so. That did not sound so easy to me. Nonetheless, we had a large and energetic group gathering at the foot of the trail. The skies were overcast and threatened rain, but we were ready—backpacks loaded, hearts full, and minds eager to get started.

As we waited for the last of our group to arrive, I wandered over to some fallen trees and broke off a branch to use as a hiking stick. I was not really much of an outdoorsman, but when I hiked, I always liked having a stick. As I returned to the group, I got the expected harassment from the teens: "Hey, Ron, are you going to carry that stick with you the whole way?" "Man, your arms are going to be tired." "I guess the old man has to have a walking stick!" "Hope you don't trip over your stick, Ron!"

Ignoring the barbs of my so-called brothers and sisters in Christ, and armed with my trusty stick, I headed for the trail. Before we began, Karen led us in prayer. We were reminded that the hike was symbolic of life's journey. We were asked to think not only of life's physical journey but also of our own spiritual journey.

It did not take long for me to realize that I was very happy to have my hiking stick. Most of our hike seemed to be straight uphill, and were it not for the assistance of my stick, I would have struggled even more. It soon became apparent that we were in for a long day.

One of my fellow adults slipped and fell. No harm was done other than a little embarrassment. Glad I have my stick, I thought to myself. As we trudged along, the stick led my way, moving branches, digging into the ground to give me footing, helping me pull myself up the hills.

Finally, after hours of walking, we reached a plateau of sorts. We stopped and rested. Karen reminded us that life, at times, can be difficult. How good it feels when you get past those difficult moments. She was so right. As we felt the cool breeze blowing through the trees and took in the beautiful view from atop the mountain, the difficult hike seemed to be fading from memory a bit. The difficult journey made us appreciate our beautiful surroundings even more.

We were promised the rest of the hike would be much easier, mostly downhill. Just like life, we were over the hump—for a while anyway. As I moved rapidly down the trail, I realized Karen was right. We were moving along, and it was much, much easier. Something just did not feel right to me though. I felt as if I had left something behind. I realized I had left my hiking stick at our resting spot. It was not really necessary to have it now, but I had grown attached to it. So I backtracked and retrieved the stick.

The rest of the hike was fairly uneventful and quite a bit more pleasant than the first part. We finally reached our destination and sat down for our long-awaited lunch. It was midafternoon by now, and we were all more than ready for our slightly dented peanut-butter-and-jelly sandwiches. It had been a long and difficult hike, but it was fun, and everyone had enjoyed it in spite of its difficulty.

As we prepared to leave, a young man approached our group, asking for help. His wife had fallen and injured her ankle, and he was not sure where he was on the trail. Had God sent him as a small test? Of course we were willing to help. Karen and I led him to the end of the trail, where he telephoned for assistance. The rest of the group soon caught up with us. I asked my wife if she had retrieved my stick. Unfortunately, she had not. I wanted to go back and look for it, but it was late and we had to get our group home. I felt disappointed that I did not have my stick as a souvenir of the occasion.

As we gathered at the end of the trail, I looked on the ground, and there it was! I grabbed that stick up like it was a long lost friend. I later found out that one of the college students on the hike had picked up the stick and carried it for me. I thought about the hike and the stick many times that week and planned to share my story with the youth at our next meeting.

I retold the story, recalling how I had been teased for having the stick to begin with; how the stick had helped me over the difficult parts of the trail; how when the going got easy, I forgot about my stick; how I felt something was missing without the stick; and, finally, how the stick appeared at the end of the trail. I then asked the group what they thought the stick symbolized. Their answer was God, and this was true. In our spiritual journey of life, it is God we should turn to when times are tough. And all too often we forget about God when things are going well.

For me, however, the stick represented the many friends God places in our lives, those who walk the journey with us. Many times we are ridiculed for the friends we choose. They may not be pretty enough or smart enough or rich enough. Often we are questioned as to why we chose them, just as I was questioned about the stick. But if we stand by our friends, they will be there for us in times of need. We can lean on them, just as I leaned on the stick.

Reflecting on the Story

Depending on the number of participants, you may want to create small groups to discuss these questions. Be sure to provide adequate discussion time before bringing the participants back into a large-group setting for overall feedback and response. Another option would be to provide the participants with journals and invite them to write their responses.

- Recall a time when you had to turn to someone because you were in need. Share that experience and how it felt to have someone to turn to.

- At what times do you call upon God for help? Do you pray more in good times or in tough times? Share a time when you felt the presence of God in your life.
- If you have ever felt like you were losing your faith in God, what steps did you take to recover that faith? If you have never lost your faith in God, what gives you the strength to maintain such faith?
- Share a time you gave support to someone who needed you. How did you feel knowing someone needed to lean on you for help?
- How does this story challenge you to realize your own need for support from others? from God?

Breaking Open the Message of the Story

Preparation

The following activities will assist the participants in breaking open the message of the story. Choose activities that are most appropriate for the group gathered and the time allotted.

Gather these items:

- sheets of drawing paper, one for each participant
- markers, several for each participant
- a wall-size map of the world
- magazines and newspapers, at least one for each participant
- scissors, one pair for each participant
- masking tape
- index cards, several for each participant
- pens or pencils, one for each participant

Who You Rely On

Distribute the drawing paper and markers. Invite the participants to draw a picture or symbol representing the people in their life they rely on. Allow about 10 minutes for the participants to complete the task. Then invite the participants to share the meaning of their drawings with the rest of the group.

A World of Peace and Harmony

Post a large map of the world on the wall (or on the floor). Distribute the magazines and newspapers and the scissors, and ask the participants to take a few minutes to imagine a world where all people care for one another in peace and harmony. Then ask them to look through the magazines and newspapers to find signs, symbols, words, and pictures that illustrate that idea. As they do so, invite them to come forward and tape the images on the world map. Be sure to take time to talk about what it would take for this illustration to really happen in the world (in homes, churches, communities, schools, the country, and so on). Hang the collage in a place where the participants can view it often so it can serve as a daily reminder to care for others.

Support from Others

Distribute a few index cards and a pen or pencil to each participant. Ask each individual to think of people in their lives who have helped them through life's journey and their faith journey. Invite them to write the name of each person on one of the index cards they have been provided, noting the circumstance or situation in which that person offered them support. After the participants have completed the task, invite them to break into small groups to share a little about the people they named.

Living the Story

Offer the following ideas to the participants as a way to continue the message of the story beyond the gathering. You might do this by listing all the ideas on a handout and sending it home, choosing one or two ideas to share and discuss with the participants, or listing the ideas on newsprint for review or discussion.

- Reflect on someone special in your life who has helped you through a tough time. Give that person a call in the next week to say thank you.
- Pay attention! Look for opportunities to be the hands and heart of Christ to others. Be open to allowing others to be Christ for you in your own times of need.

Praying the Story

Preparation

Gather these items for the following prayer experience:

- ○ a table
- ○ a hiking stick or tree branch
- ○ candles and matches
- ○ a copy of *The Catholic Youth Bible*™ or another Bible

Process

1. Prepare the prayer space by placing a table in the center of the room. Place the hiking stick or tree branch on the table and surround it with candles, open Bible, and so forth. Gather the participants in a circle around the table.

2. Invite the participants to take a moment to silently reflect on family members, friends, acquaintances, and even strangers who have offered help or support during difficult times. Then ask the participants to prayerfully place the index cards from the previous activity on the table, surrounding the stick.

3. Invite the participants to pass the stick around the circle as you read the following prayer:

○ Loving and gracious God,
We come together this day with grateful hearts.
You have placed many special people in our lives to help us each day.
We thank you for each and every one of them.
We ask you to keep us ever mindful of our family and friends
   and to never take them for granted.
Give us the strength and wisdom to be there for them, just as they are
   there for us.
Amen.

4. Invite the participants to join you in praying the following intercession, by responding, "Lord, we thank you" to each phrase you read.

○   For the gift of our family, . . .
    For the gift of our friends, . . .
    For the gift of our Church, . . .
    For the gift of faith, . . .
    In gratitude for the support we get during difficult times, . . .
    In thanksgiving for having people to share the happy times with, . . .
    In thanksgiving for the gift of Jesus, . . .
    Lord, we ask these things in the name of your Son, Jesus Christ,
        who is always there for us.
    Amen.

5. To conclude, invite the participants to retrieve their index cards and place them in their purses or wallets as a reminder to be thankful for those who are "the stick" to them.

Chapter 9

The Hike

Key Themes

- Helping others in need is the Christian way to live.
- Often when we are burdened with problems, we think we are unable to help others.
- Reaching out to help even when we are in distress ourselves can actually reduce our own burden.

Scripture Connections

- Matthew 27:32 (Simon of Cyrene carries the cross.)
- John 13:12–16 (Jesus washes his disciples' feet.)
- Romans 12:9–16 (Serve the Lord with devotion.)

The Story

You may want to read the story "The Stick," in chapter 8, if you have not already done so.

Offer the following introduction before telling the story:

- A lesson of service is learned along the way as hikers take turns carrying one another's backpacks and sleeping bags. Sometimes to make our burden lighter, we need to take on the burden of others.

The World Youth Day gathering our group attended was to end with Pope John Paul II celebrating Sunday morning Mass. On Saturday the hundreds of thousands attending were to make a short hike to the site of that night's vigil service. I tried to keep my spirits and energy level high, but I had a great feeling of nervousness as our long-awaited and much-dreaded hike approached. Our group members wore small backpacks and carried sleeping bags and other essentials in plastic garbage bags. Because most of us were inexperienced hikers trying to prepare for all situations, we had packed way too much and were severely over-loaded.

Not knowing how far we had to travel made our journey even more diffi-cult. We tried singing songs, talking, and praying—anything to pass the time and take our minds off the ever-increasing burdens on our backs and in our arms. I was pretty tired from the week's events, and my choice of shoes was a mistake, as my feet hurt even before I started the walk.

As expected, our group members, young and old alike, began the obligatory whining. Half in jest, one of the girls, Krista, came by and asked if I would carry her sleeping bag. She was shocked when I answered with a resounding yes.

She refused, of course, but I insisted, telling her that when I got tired, she could carry mine. She was delighted, and I felt a burst of energy. By adding her load, mine actually felt lighter. I decided that if anyone asked me to carry some-thing for them, I would not refuse. And so it went, person after person coming over and asking me, kiddingly, when I would carry his or her backpack. One by one, I helped carry someone else's bags, sometimes for just a minute or two and sometimes longer.

The more I carried someone else's pack, the stronger I got. I then began to notice others doing the same thing. As I glanced up ahead, I saw Krista carrying her mother's pack. She ended up carrying it nearly the whole way.

Another bit of inspiration came from a fellow hiker who asked us to think of Jesus carrying the cross. Just how heavy was that cross? How far did Jesus have to go? Why were we complaining? At the end of our journey was a campground that would be filled with thousands of people celebrating with music, fellow-ship, and prayer. At the end of Jesus's journey was death on the cross.

The hike went much faster as I carried bag after bag, sometimes two or three. Several of the young people helped me with mine as well. In the midst of this great spiritual week, I was again struck by the lessons that can be learned in such a routine situation.

Often in life we are burdened by problems. Perhaps *often* is not the correct word. Sometimes it seems we are constantly burdened by life's challenges. Chores to do, tests to take, too much homework, difficulties with loved ones, ill-ness, death, just trying to fit in—all these are loaded into the backpacks we carry around each day. We are so concerned about our own problems that we often have a hard time thinking of helping others.

Somehow if we do ever reach out to another and ask if we can help, our own burden becomes lighter. Perhaps we realize that no matter how great our own needs, there is always someone whose needs are greater. Whatever sadness or tragedy befalls us, someone else has experienced a similar or greater tragedy. When we begin to reach out to others and help them, our own burdens may seem less significant and thus begin to be lifted. Taking on another's burden may actually lighten the load for both people. Maybe our load is not really lightened, but our spirit is lifted and we are stronger because we are living the true spirit of Christianity: helping others. Then, an amazing thing can happen. The person we helped may be willing to help another, and that one another, and another, and on it goes.

In some of my darkest times, I try to remember the lesson of this day. It is a simple one, but it can be easily forgotten when the backpack of life becomes overloaded. Often I am not the one who is doing the reaching out, but rather a friend is reaching out to me. As soon as I feel the relief of my friend's helping hand, I am strengthened and ready to do the same for others.

It is an old lesson: the Golden Rule. I do not profess to have thought of it first. But when life sneaks up on us and we have the chance to live it firsthand, we can only hope we are ready and paying attention. We should pay attention even if our shoes are killing our feet, even if we're in the middle of nowhere (or Colorado) walking with hundreds of thousands of people from around the world. Pay attention. Jesus might wander up next to you and ask, "How about helping me carry this?" I hope I am ready and willing to give the right answer. I hope you are as well.

Reflecting on the Story

Depending on the number of participants, you may want to create small groups to discuss these questions. Be sure to provide adequate discussion time before bringing the participants back into a large-group setting for overall feedback and response. Another option would be to provide the participants with journals and invite them to write their responses.

- Recall a low point for you. What were your thoughts at that time? How did you get help from others to deal with your situation?
- Reflect on a time you helped a friend or family member through a tough period in his or her life. How did helping make you feel?
- What helps you get out of your bad moods? Share things that inspire, motivate, and help you when you are depressed.
- Think of people you know who need a helping hand right now. How can you help them? Think of specific things you can do to help out.
- Reflect on whether you think Jesus ever felt burdened by his duty. How did he handle the burden?

Breaking Open the Message of the Story

Preparation

The following activities will assist the participants in breaking open the message of the story. Choose activities that are most appropriate for the group gathered and the time allotted.

Gather these items:

- children's puzzles (simple puzzles with a few large pieces that are easy to put together), one for every two participants

- blindfolds, one for every two participants

- pieces of cord, one for every two participants

- copies of *The Catholic Youth Bible*™ or another Bible, one for each small group of four or five

Working Together

Divide the large group into pairs. Give each pair a children's puzzle, a blindfold, and a piece of cord. Ask one person in each pair to tie the cord around his or her partner's wrists. Then have the bound person put on the blindfold and try to put together the puzzle with no help from his or her partner. Give a few minutes for each person to try, and then stop for a discussion of what frustrations each experienced. Next, tell the pairs they can work together to solve the puzzle. After all the pairs have finished their puzzles, discuss how each team worked together to solve the puzzle.

In Simon's Shoes

Divide the large group into small groups of four to five. Distribute the bibles and ask each group to read Matthew 27:32 and reflect on the role of Simon of Cyrene. The groups are to prepare a skit that re-enacts the events leading up to Simon's carrying the cross for Jesus. The skits are to be from the perspective of Simon. The groups can consider these questions in putting together their skits: How did Simon happen to be there that day? What was he thinking when he was forced to carry the cross? Be sure the groups show how Simon interacted with Jesus. You might also ask the groups to demonstrate how Simon may have felt after he carried the cross.

Sharing the Burden

Ask the participants to stand with their arms extended straight out in front of them. Tell them to remain standing until their arms drop. Then they must be seated. The last person standing wins. Along the way, make things more difficult by placing books on the back of some participants' hands to weigh them down. At some point, invite the participants to find a partner and rest their hands on that person's hands. When the activity is over, ask the participants to share how they felt during the activity. Be prepared to connect back to the message of the story. Did having a partner help to share the burden?

Living the Story

Offer the following ideas to the participants as a way to continue the message of the story beyond the gathering. You might do this by listing all the ideas on a handout and sending it home, choosing one or two ideas to share and discuss with the participants, or listing the ideas on newsprint for review or discussion.

- Volunteer to help at home. Ask your mom or dad if you can help out with something. Do this cheerfully. Do it even if you are busy (especially if you are busy).
- Volunteer to help at school. Do you have a friend who could use some help with a project or a subject? Volunteer to help in whatever way you can.
- Surprise your teacher. Offer to help with one of his or her tasks—carrying books, straightening bookshelves, tidying the room.
- The next time you see trash in the hallway or on the school grounds, pick it up. Organize a clean-up day for your school.
- Research peer ministry groups. Volunteer at an organization that helps troubled teens.

Praying the Story

Preparation

Gather these items for the following prayer experience:

- ○ a table
- ○ one large candle; several small candles, one for each participant; and matches

○ index cards, one for each participant

○ a marker

○ a copy of *The Catholic Youth Bible*™ or another Bible

Process

1. Gather the group in the prayer space. In the center of the table, place the large candle and surround it by smaller candles. On individual index cards, write the names of each participant. Place one index card under each small candle.

2. Light the large candle and ask the group to reflect on Jesus as the light of the world.

3. Invite a participant to proclaim Matthew 22:34–40. Allow a few moments of silence to follow.

4. Approach the prayer table and invite one of the participants to do so as well. Then light a small candle from the larger one saying, "(participant name), you are the light of the world." Then give the candle to the participant. Have that participant call up another person, hand a lit candle to him or her, and say the same thing. Continue this process until all the participants have received a candle. You may choose to play music during this part (Kathy Troccoli's "Go Light Your World" is a good choice.)

5. Conclude with the following prayer or words of your own choosing:

○ O, loving and gracious God,
>   we come to you today with willing and open hearts.
> Keep us ever mindful of the needs of others.
> We also ask that you help us remain open to the help that others
>   offer us.
> Help us follow the example of Simon, who helped Jesus on the
>   road to Calvary.
> Inspire us to be willing to help even in times when our own needs
>   and selfishness may get in the way.
> We ask a special blessing on those of us who have gathered here today.
> Keep us strong and always willing to reach out.
> We ask all these things in the name of your Son, Jesus,
>   whose example we strive to follow.
> Amen.

Chapter 10

Caller ID

Key Themes

- God supports and encourages us in our endeavors even when we are not aware of it.
- Working together toward a common goal unifies people.
- When we are overwhelmed and anxious, God reminds us that we are never alone.

Scripture Connections

- Acts of the Apostles 2:43–47 (The Christian community is powerful.)
- Romans 12:3–11 (We have many gifts but are one body, and we belong to one another in Christ.)
- Hebrews 2:1–4 (Pay attention!)

The Story

Offer the following introduction before telling the story:

> o How often do we ask for a sign from God to let us know that what we are doing is the right thing? In this story, a family receives a sign that encourages them and supports them as they pursue a common goal.

A few years ago, my brother, George, had this great notion to open a restaurant. His enthusiasm for the project was so contagious that it quickly spread to everyone in the family. He had dreamed it, shared the idea with our nephews who helped him think it into a realistic possibility, and set about to make it happen. His passion ignited a fire in each of us.

From the beginning, I had a strong sense of what was fueling his desire to take on this monumental project. George wanted our family to focus on a common goal and move in the same direction together. At the time, we were living in different states and seeing one another only a few times a year. Our family bonds were stretched to the limits. In George's mind, this restaurant would give us a special place to gather and reinforce our feelings of kinship. Our children would be working together and learning to be a family that depended on one another.

There was a second reason for this project. George was looking for a way to honor our parents and our heritage. That was the piece that sold all of us on the idea. We felt charged with the responsibility of sharing the characteristics of hospitality and goodness that our parents taught us. That was the heart of the dream.

A business venture like this looks much easier on paper and in theory than in reality. A mind-boggling amount of money and time is needed just to get things started. It takes diplomacy to work with the "professionals," and it requires great patience and dedication. After several months of nail-biting anxiety, we were ready to build the restaurant that would be known by our family name.

Something very curious happened while all the planning was going on. One day I called my sister to check in. This is nothing special; we call each other nearly every day. But when I called this particular time, she noticed that our father's name appeared on her caller ID. Yet our dad had been dead for more than thirty years. I have never had a phone registered in his name, and my married name in no way resembles his. In the twenty-six years I had been married, nothing like this had ever happened! My sister and I thought it must be a bizarre coincidence, so I hung up and tried again. Same result. Our dad's name appeared on her screen. This was very strange. I called my brothers to see which name showed up on their phones. Mine. I called my children. My name. I called friends. Again, my name. This quirk occurred only when I called my sister.

Baffled and looking for answers, I called the phone company and explained the situation. The technician listened in stunned silence before admitting, "Ma'am, I just don't have a clue what's going on." This went on for several months. Every time I called my sister's home, dad's name appeared. Also during this time, I began to get random phone calls from people asking for my father. When I would answer that he had passed away many years ago, the callers seemed puzzled. This was the hot topic of conversation for many months. I mentioned it to anyone and everyone, hoping someone might have a logical explanation. No one did.

Finally, it occurred to us that just maybe this was a sign from our parents that what we were doing pleased them, that bringing the family together to focus on one goal was a very good thing.

Usually I am wary and a little afraid of things that have no explanation. But from the first time it happened, I felt encouraged and excited. I knew this was something special. When the restaurant finally opened, those feelings proved true and right. Everyone had a place and a purpose in this family business. Our children realized talents and gifts they never knew they possessed. They learned to work together to produce a beautiful product, guiding and teaching one another from their deep pool of skills. The greatest benefit was that they were able to grow their childhood relationships to maturity. They have become more than just brothers and sisters and cousins; they are real friends. They discovered how much they love one another.

The restaurant has become a place for us to celebrate the moments of our lives with one another and with the new and treasured friends who have become family to us. These are the things that endure. These are the things that matter.

One thing I have learned from this experience is to pay close attention to the signs. Sometimes such signs are obvious; other times they are mysterious and difficult to explain or understand. God speaks to us in many ways. We believe we were fortunate to recognize this sign. Just imagine the ones we don't see!

Reflecting on the Story

Depending on the number of participants, you may want to create small groups to discuss these questions. Be sure to provide adequate discussion time before bringing the participants back into a large-group setting for overall feedback and response. Another option would be to provide the participants with journals and invite them to write their responses.

- Describe a time when you have had a similar experience with signs.
- Describe a time when you or your family have prayed for a sign.
- In what kind of circumstances have you found yourself very anxious and nervous? What helped you get through those difficult experiences?
- This story is about renewing and strengthening family ties. How does your family grow and nurture its relationships over time?

Breaking Open the Message of the Story

Preparation

The following activities will assist the participants in breaking open the message of the story. Choose activities that are most appropriate for the group gathered and the time allotted.

Gather these items:

- sheets of newsprint, one for each small group of four or five for each activity
- markers of various colors, one for each participant
- copies of *The Catholic Youth Bible*™ or another Bible, one for each small group of four or five
- balloons, one for each small group of four or five
- small votive candles, one for each participant, and matches

Coincidence or Not?

Divide the large group into small groups of four or five people. Provide each group with a sheet of newsprint and a marker. Then make the following comments in your own words.

- A coincidence is an event that, although random and accidental, seems to have been planned or arranged. Take a few moments to think of events in your own experience that you considered coincidental. When everyone has had enough time, share these in your small group to determine common characteristics (unexpected, unexplainable, and so on). Have someone in your group write these characteristics on the newsprint.

When all the groups have compiled their newsprint lists, ask someone in each group to present to the large group. Then, as a large group, compare and contrast each list. Conclude the activity by discussing the following question: Do you think the experiences described were random coincidences, or do you believe they could have been the work of the Holy Spirit trying to get your attention?

Signs and Wonders

Divide the large group into small groups of four or five people. Distribute a
Bible, a sheet of newsprint, and a few markers to each group. Note that many
signs and wonders were attributed to Jesus and his disciples. Tell the groups
that they will have 10 minutes to make a list on newsprint of as many of these
wonders as they can find in the New Testament. Offer a few examples, such
as the Holy Spirit resting above the heads of the disciples as flames of fire at
Pentecost. That was a symbol of the gifts the Holy Spirit was giving to each person, empowering him to go among the people to spread the Good News (see
Acts of the Apostles 2:1–4). Another example is Saul's being struck by a bright
light and left blinded when he was persecuting the followers of Jesus. His tem-
porary blindness was a sign of the suffering he must endure as a converted fol-
lower of Jesus (see Acts of the Apostles 9:1–9).

When the 10 minutes are up, come back together in the large group and take
turns describing the purpose or meaning of these signs and wonders.

Identities and Symbols

Divide the large group into small groups of four or five people. Distribute a
sheet of newsprint and a different-color marker to each participant in the small
group. Note that the story they heard was also about the importance of work-
ing together. Ask the small groups to spend a few minutes learning about one
another's personal identity by asking questions that may help them to know
one another better. Here some examples of good questions they can ask:
• What are your interests?
• Do you have special talents in art? music?
• What are your hobbies? favorite classes in school?
• Where were you born?
• Have you traveled outside of the United States?
The object is to understand each person's identity in order to create a composite
group identity. Once the group members have a general idea of who each person in their group is, their task is to create a symbol that represents their entire
group. Each group member chooses a different-color marker to represent himself
or herself as an individual. The group decides together what their symbol will
be, and each person uses his or her own color to contribute to the drawing. Give
the groups an opportunity to explain their symbols to the large group.

A Common Goal

Have a little fun with this one. Divide the large group into small groups of eight to ten. Instruct the small groups to stand in a circle and hold hands. Their task is to work together to keep a balloon from touching the ground. They must not release one another's hands. The leaders call out a body part that they can touch the balloon with (maybe wrists only) and releases a balloon in the center of each circle. To make it more difficult, change the body part every few minutes. Use heads, elbows, knees, chests. There is no winner or loser. The purpose is to work together to keep the balloon flying. Then conduct a discussion on the importance of working together toward a common goal.

Living the Story

Offer the following ideas to the participants as a way to continue the message of the story beyond the gathering. You might do this by listing all the ideas on a handout and sending it home, choosing one or two ideas to share and discuss with the participants, or listing the ideas on newsprint for review or discussion.

- Coincidence is God's way of being anonymous. Be alert! Pay close attention to people, events, and experiences. It may be God trying to get in touch with you!
- Be open and willing to be a vessel for the Holy Spirit to use in order that you may be the sign prayed for in another person's life.
- Be a team player. We use our talents best when we join them with the talents of others to achieve a goal that benefits the team (or family, or group, and so on).
- Write a letter or make a phone call to a relative with whom you have lost touch. Pave the way to renewing this relationship.

Praying the Story

Preparation

Gather these items for the following prayer experience:

- ○ a large candle; several small candles, one for each participant; and matches
- ○ a copy of *The Catholic Youth Bible*™ or another Bible

Process

1. Place the large candle in the center of your prayer space, surrounding it with the small candles. Invite the participants to join you, asking them to sit in a circle around the candles. Ask them to sit in quiet reverence as you light the large candle. Invite one participant to come forward to light a smaller candle, and then, one by one going around the circle, allow the others to do the same.

2. When the candles are all lit, ask a participant to proclaim Romans 12:4–8. Allow a few moments of silence to follow. Then ask the participants to reflect quietly for a moment about the special gift they personally bring to this group to make it complete.

3. Going around the circle, invite each participant to share in one or two words what that gift is.

4. Conclude by inviting the participants to join in praying the Glory Be.

Chapter 11

The Stick Lives On

Key Themes

- God is always there for us.
- The faith journey is a never-ending experience.
- Faith in God will give us strength.

Scripture Connections

- Psalm 18:1–3 (God is my rock.)
- Matthew 28:16–20 (I am always with you.)
- 2 Timothy 4:6–8 ("I have kept the faith.")

The Story

You may want to read the story "The Stick," in chapter 8, as background for this story.
Offer the following introduction before telling the story:

> ○ Though there are times when our faith wavers or we try to carry on without God, it is good to know that God is always there for us. After we overcome the challenge, we may find that our faith has been strengthened and that we are ready to take on the next part of our journey. In this story, a simple stick becomes a symbol of strength and of survival that is possible only with faith in God.

After months and months of preparation, prayer, and fundraising, our group's trip to World Youth Day in Denver, Colorado, was finally here. The anticipation and excitement of gathering with Catholics from all over the world was almost too much to bear. We would soon be getting on the bus for our 30-hour ride to Denver.

We had been drilled on how to pack, what to take, and what to leave behind. So as my family and I gathered our luggage, we checked our list—suitcase, backpack, sleeping bag, and pillow. Four people, four items. That was it, except for one more thing. I still had to decide about the stick.

The stick had become so important since a hike our group had taken last spring. By now most members of the church had heard the legend of the stick. What should I do about the stick on the trip?

I sat it by the luggage and at the last minute decided to grab it. I'll at least bring it to the bus to show everyone. When we got to the bus, I decided there wouldn't be any harm in bringing the stick along for the ride. I would just slip it into the luggage compartment of the bus and keep it in my room . . . no problem.

We stacked our luggage outside the bus for the driver to load. When he saw the stick, Gary, our driver, gave me a funny look. He was immediately assured by several members of the group that the stick was very special and that there was a rather long story attached to it. He nodded his head, not really understanding, and said he would like to hear the story sometime.

The bus ride was long and tiresome to say the least. Somewhere along the way, I told Gary the story of the stick. He seemed amused, but his face showed an appreciation for the meaning behind the story. Nearly a day and a half after we started our trip, we finally arrived in Denver.

During the entire week, the stick remained in the motel room. Each day we left our room knowing we would not return for twelve to fourteen hours. One carried only what was necessary: the lighter the load, the easier the day would be. So there was no room and no need for the stick. But still, it had made the journey, and having it there made us feel good.

The conclusion to the World Youth Day celebration was Sunday morning Mass with Pope John Paul II. This was preceded by a Saturday night vigil service at the Mass site. After the vigil service, all the participants were to camp out in anticipation of Mass the next morning. So on Saturday morning, we packed up and readied for the hike. Fortunately the length of our walk was only 2 to 3 miles, not the 13 originally anticipated.

The buses unloaded, and we gathered our backpacks and sleeping bags, preparing for our hike. As we stood around getting ready to pray, I heard Gary calling me: "Hey, Ronnie, what about the stick?" Gary held it high in the air. I had not planned on taking the stick on the hike. I did not need it, and truthfully, I was glad it had survived this long without being damaged. With several hundred thousand people around, anything could happen. What if the stick got broken or lost? In spite of all these thoughts, I gazed at the stick held high and knew I had no choice. I took the stick from Gary and got ready for the hike.

The group gathered around, and we remembered the meaning behind the stick. The stick supported me on a previous group hike and had now become a symbol for how our group supported one another during our times of preparation for this trip.

We decided then that the stick would be our focal point on this hike, as it would be close to impossible to keep thirty people together in the midst of tens of thousands who would be making the hike to the park. So we would take turns carrying the stick at the front of the group. The leader's job would be to hold the stick high so that all the others would know where our group was. I started the journey carrying the stick, but only for a short while. Almost immediately several of the young people wanted to carry the stick. It became an honor to carry the stick, but one could do so only if one knew its meaning.

And so the hike progressed, the stick being passed from one member of our group to another. I had to banish one boy from carrying the stick for not showing it proper respect. The stick was certainly not meant to be used as a weapon. Later, on his second opportunity, he showed proper respect. Even then I was still amazed at how much that stick meant to me and the entire group. Of course, there was more in store for the stick.

We set up camp in the open area with thousands around us. Hesitantly, I agreed to let the stick serve as a prop for a makeshift tent. I cringed as one of the boys wrapped masking tape around it. At least the stick was being useful, proving again its versatility and dependability in times of need.

At the conclusion of Mass, the half million people stood in reverence as the Pope prepared to give us his final blessing. Almost everyone in the crowd stood with crosses, rosaries, holy cards held aloft to receive this most special blessing. I gathered my own items up and held them aloft. Held firmly in my left hand, raised upward for the Pope's blessing, was the stick.

As I stood there, I thought about the stick and its many meanings. By being with me every step of this fantastic spiritual journey, I wondered if the stick represented the Holy Spirit, our guide and our inspiration. It most certainly was representative of God — always there for us, even when we don't notice. Whether the stick was left behind in the room, shoved under the bus, or passed from person to person, it was always there. So it is with God.

In the ensuing craziness to return to the bus, there were many trials and troubles. Our group was separated, and I was one of the last ones to return to the bus with my wife and four of our young people. Two members of our group had been taken for medical attention because of the altitude and heat. It had been a difficult end to a spiritually rewarding, yet physically demanding, experience. As for the stick, no one seemed to know if it had made it back, but I was assured it was safely tucked away beneath the bus. Our long journey home began, and I pondered the fate of the stick. I pondered my own fate, knowing I had been changed forever by this experience.

Finally, our agonizing bus trip home ended, and exhausted but spiritually renewed, we were greeted by hundreds of friends and family. I was relieved to find the stick had made the journey home beneath the bus. This fragile stick had survived riding for many hours under the bus, spending a week in Denver, being passed from person to person on the hike, and being used as a tent stake, and it was still intact, stronger than ever. We too can endure hardships, journeys, and trials and emerge not broken but stronger. The stick now became a symbol of strength, of survival, that is possible only with faith in God. After all, the stick had survived a long and perilous journey, a journey that had begun on a trail in a state park in Alabama and ended in a state park at the foot of the Rocky Mountains in Colorado.

For me, this journey had begun many years before, when I was baptized into the Catholic faith as an infant. Now, as I gathered up the stick to return home, I realized my journey was truly just beginning.

Reflecting on the Story

Depending on the number of participants, you may want to create small groups to discuss these questions. Be sure to provide adequate discussion time before bringing the participants back into a large-group setting for overall feedback and response. Another option would be to provide the participants with journals and invite them to write their responses.

- Reflect on times you may have set God aside in your life. How were you able to reconnect with God?
- Discuss the things that guide you to live life the way you think it should be lived. Who or what in your life has helped you stay focused on the right path?
- Reflect on your own spiritual journey. Share the earliest experience you can remember of church or God. How has your attitude toward church changed since then? your attitude toward God?
- Think about the goals you have set for your life. What spiritual goals do you have? How do you intend to attain those goals?
- Reflect on challenges in your life. How has your faith helped you overcome those challenges? Share how you felt after the experiences had passed. How did overcoming one challenge enable you to meet the next?

Breaking Open the Message of the Story

Preparation

The following activities will assist the participants in breaking open the message of the story. Choose activities that are most appropriate for the group gathered and the time allotted.

Gather these items:

- ○ sheets of blank paper, one for each participant
- ○ markers, several for each participant
- ○ playing cards, one deck for each small group of five or six
- ○ a roll of Scotch tape
- ○ a copy of *The Catholic Youth Bible*™ or another Bible, one for each small group of five or six

Spiritual Journey

Give each participant a piece of paper and some markers. Ask them to use symbols to depict their own spiritual journey. In the center of the page have them create a representation of themselves. Surrounding that representation tell them to draw symbols or pictures that represent those things that support and challenge their spiritual growth. When everyone is finished, ask the participants to share the meaning of their drawings with the group.

God Gives Us Strength

Divide the large group into smaller groups of five or six and give each small group a deck of cards. Tell the groups they are to build a house of cards that symbolizes themselves, their family, and their friends. Will this be a sturdy house? Will they choose to use lots of cards or just a few? Will the house be tall and grand or short and simple? Quietly give one group a roll of Scotch tape to help them build their house. Do this without the other groups knowing. Allow 5 to 10 minutes for the groups to get their house of cards as sturdy as possible. Then have each group share what it has done. The group with the tape goes last. Discuss how God's presence in our lives strengthens us (like the Scotch tape did for the card house) and all our relationships.

Interview with a Biblical Character

Divide the large group into smaller groups of five or six and give each group a Bible. Tell each group to locates a passage in the Bible where someone kept the faith despite adversity. Then have the group discuss the person and prepare an interview with the person. Ask one group member to serve as moderator, and another to represent the Bible character chosen. The interviews can take place within the small groups, or they can be shared with the large group.

Living the Story

Offer the following ideas to the participants as a way to continue the message of the story beyond the gathering. You might do this by listing all the ideas on a handout and sending it home, choosing one or two ideas to share and discuss with the participants, or listing the ideas on newsprint for review or discussion.

- Strengthen your spiritual life by reading the Bible. Tonight choose one chapter of the Bible to read. Resolve to read the Bible more often and to obtain sources to help you with your study.
- Strengthen your prayer life by praying more. Resolve to pray more often. Pray in the car on the way to school. Pray before you fall asleep. Pray.
- Live your faith by getting involved at church. Read the bulletin. Find out what is happening. Attend events.
- Make a new friend. Find someone that needs a friend and reach out. Listen to his or her story. Share your own.
- Thank God for those who have helped you on your spiritual journey.

Praying the Story

Process

1. Gather the participants in the prayer space and invite them to sit or lie comfortably. Observe a moment of quiet and then proceed.

2. Ask the group to close their eyes and listen as you speak. Ask them to breathe deeply and slowly and follow the instructions as you give them. Speak slowly and deliberately, allowing long pauses. You may choose to have soothing music playing during this prayer session.

3. First ask the participants to relax their bodies, one part at a time. Start with the feet, and then move up to the legs, hips, stomach, arms, and so on.

Pause after naming each body part to give the participants time to relax. Remind them to breathe deeply.

4. Recite the following meditation or something similar:

o Imagine that you are on a large, open plain, and you are all alone. Picture the scene, the sky, the sun, and the clouds. What can you hear? What do you see around you? You see a mountain in the distance, and you begin to walk toward it. You are drawn to it, and know you must climb it. What are your thoughts as you move forward? Are you nervous . . . excited . . . curious? Finally you reach the mountain and begin your climb. Feel the rocks beneath your feet. The hill becomes steeper, and soon you are climbing almost straight uphill. You are clinging to the side of the mountain. Your feet are slipping. You are barely holding on, but you continue to climb, drawn to the top. You feel yourself weakening. Feel your arms tiring, your feet slipping, and the wind battering you. How long can you hold on? Then you feel a hand grasp your wrist. You are secure. You look up, but the sun blinds your sight. Who has grabbed you? Who has saved you? You feel a second hand grab you, and you are pulled upward. You know you have the strength to climb to the plateau, and you pull yourself up and can finally rest. You look to see who helped you, but no one is there. You are all alone. Feel the wind blowing, the warmth of the sun on your face. You turn . . . and there is another hill to climb. What do you do?

5. Observe a few moments of silence, and then ask the group members to share any thoughts they have about the experience. Spend just a few minutes on this. Do not delve too deeply into the experience unless individuals wish to share more.

6. Conclude by offering the following prayer:

o Loving and gracious God,
We come to you today to ask for your ever-present guidance
as we travel our life's journey.
Help us to stay strong, to keep the faith,
and to continue on in spite of adversity.
When life's times and troubles get us down, we pray that our faith
will strengthen us to meet those challenges and that by
overcoming those challenges, our faith will be even stronger.
We ask these prayers in the name of your faithful and loyal Son, Jesus,
who stands by our side to show us the way.
Amen.

Chapter 12

A Seat on the Bus

Key Themes

- Social injustice is a prevailing evil.
- Unjust laws must be challenged.
- Peaceful conflict can effect positive change.

Scripture Connections

- Matthew 7:1–5 (Do not judge, or you too will be judged.)
- Galatians 3:26–29 (You are all sons and daughters of God.)
- James 2:1–9 (Do not make distinctions amongst yourselves.)

The Story

Before the participants arrive, divide the meeting space into two distinct sections, front and back. You can do this with masking tape, rope, or any other means you may think of. As the participants enter, assign each one a seat in either section, but do not offer them an explanation. For the duration of the gathering, do not allow those in the back to come forward for any reason. Keep the areas strictly separated and let your demeanor and speech show favoritism for the participants in the front.

Offer the following introduction before telling the story.

     o   In this story, a frightening experience of social injustice and bigotry has a profound effect on a young person and awakens in her the desire and commitment to live a life of justice and peace.

I started school in 1960. It was the era of the civil rights movement in the United States, and Alabama was the boiling pot. Segregation was the fabric of the South at that time. There were separate bathrooms for whites and blacks; separate water fountains for whites and blacks; and schools, restaurants, hotels, and churches were segregated. At that time, slavery had been abolished for nearly one hundred years, but the attitude that "white was right" remained and hung on fiercely, especially in the South. It was a matter of tradition. It was not unusual at that time to hear someone say, "If God wanted us to mix, he'd have made us all the same." I heard it then and, sadly, I sometimes still hear it now.

It is difficult to say what it felt like to be a child growing up under the cloud of racism. My family lived in a nice, middle-class, white neighborhood only one block from an African American neighborhood. I met most African American people while playing in my yard as they walked past our house from the bus stop. I remember thinking how polite they were, always greeting me with "Evenin', Ma'am"; tipping a hat to me; or giving me a nod, as if I were much older and had earned that respect. I always wanted to play with the African American children passing my yard, but their parents pulled them along quickly, and I never even learned their names.

Some nights there would be a knock on our front door. My mother would answer it to find someone, usually an elderly African American man, asking for food. She would invite him in and seat him at the kitchen table as she fixed him something to eat. While he ate, she would prepare a to-go bag full of sandwiches and snacks. I learned from her that we feed the hungry, that we take care of one another. It made no sense to me that she could show such kindness to people who were not allowed to be our neighbors. It made no sense to her either. Looking back, I think my mother challenged those laws best by welcoming those strangers to her table. There were many other people who challenged those laws too. One of the more well known was Mrs. Rosa Parks. Her actions resulted in the Montgomery, Alabama, bus boycott that changed the course of history and brought racism to the national stage. On December 1, 1955, Mrs. Parks and three other passengers took seats in the fifth row of a bus, the first row blacks (according to the law) were allowed to occupy. When the white rows filled and a white man was left standing, the bus driver approached Mrs. Parks and her companions and asked them to move. Three of the women gave up their seats, but Mrs. Parks refused. She was arrested.

Eventually, forced segregation on buses became an issue before the United States Supreme Court. The date was November 13, 1956, nearly one year from the one-day boycott.

In 1960, a few years after Mrs. Parks' brave act cracked open the evil of segregation, a similar incident happened to me. My sister and I rode a bus to school each day. One morning, as usual, the bus was overloaded with people. At a stop near our school, a group came on and shoved its way to the back. An elderly

African American woman who seemed shaky on her feet stood, holding onto the back of a seat for balance, so I got up and offered her my seat. She gratefully accepted. At the next stop, the bus driver came back and told her to get up and give me back my seat. I remember the hateful tone of the driver's voice. Through the eyes of a six-year-old, I saw him as a big bully. The weary woman sighed and got up. She patted my shoulder gently as we passed each other. I slumped back into the seat and buried my head in my sister's lap, trying to muffle my tears and hide my embarrassment. Looking back on the incident, I still wonder why the adults on the bus remained silent. Surely they knew this was wrong. Did their silence mean they supported the bus driver's attitude?

I've never forgotten that day. It was my first real taste of injustice, and it painted for me a clear picture of what evil looks like. Changing the world requires changing hearts and attitudes. Each time we take a stand against injustice, no matter how small, we become advocates for peace and justice. Each of us has the capacity to change the world, just like Mrs. Rosa Parks, one small choice at a time.

Reflecting on the Story

Depending on the number of participants, you may want to create small groups to discuss these questions. Be sure to provide adequate discussion time before bringing the participants back into a large-group setting for overall feedback and response. Another option would be to provide the participants with journals and invite them to write their responses.

- What has been your own experience of, or witness to, injustice?
- Describe a time when you felt unable to challenge injustice because of your age or lack of experience.
- In what ways did Jesus respond to injustice?
- What type of injustice would you be willing to risk arrest for in order to challenge it?

Breaking Open the Message of the Story

Preparation

The following activities will assist the participants in breaking open the message of the story. Choose activities that are most appropriate for the group gathered and the time allotted.

Gather these items:

○ sheets of newsprint, one for each small group of five or six

○ markers, several for each small group of five or six

○ index cards, one for each participant

○ sheets of blank paper, one for each participant

○ pens or pencils, one for each participant

Discuss Segregation

Once you have read the story and invited small-group discussion, remove the barrier line you created before the gathering began, invite the participants to convene in a large group, and discuss how it felt to be segregated from one another.

Fighting Injustice

Divide the large group into small groups of five or six, and ask the small groups to pinpoint a specific injustice in their schools. Examples might include favoritism toward athletes, indifference toward minorities, or special privileges for the academically advanced. Provide a sheet of newsprint and several markers to each group, and ask the groups to develop an action plan to peacefully and fairly effect change in regard to the issue they have noted. Allow each group time to present its action plan to the large group.

Fighting Exclusion

Write on index cards common scenarios in which exclusion occurs. Examples might include a qualified person's not being hired for a job because he or she is disabled, a family's not being welcomed into a new neighborhood because it is different (nationality, race, religion), a gay teen's being taunted by a group of straight teens, and so on. Randomly distribute one card to each participant along with a blank sheet of paper and a pen or pencil. Ask them to write a response as to how they would intervene or advocate on behalf of the individual or group being discriminated against. Offer the participants the opportunity to share their reflections with the large group.

Living the Story

Offer the following ideas to the participants as a way to continue the message of the story beyond the gathering. You might do this by listing all the ideas on a handout and sending it home, choosing one or two ideas to share and discuss with the participants, or listing the ideas on newsprint for review or discussion.

- Watch the nightly news as a family. Pray together for peace, understanding, and justice.
- Be aware of what's happening around you. Make an effort, no matter how small, to make others feel important and valued. Sometimes it's as easy as saying hello.
- Vow to be an agent of justice. Practice treating others the way you want to be treated, until it becomes your habit.
- Create a prayer board where you place reminders of people and places you want to pray for daily.

Praying the Story

Preparation

Gather these items for the following prayer experience:

- small slips of paper or index cards, one for each participant
- pens or pencils, one for each participant
- a small basket

Process

1. Distribute the slips of paper or index cards and the pens or pencils. Ask the participants to jot down a prayer request or concern that centers on issues of injustice. Allow a few minutes for them to think about and write their requests. Collect the prayer petitions in a basket and place the basket prominently in the center of the group.

2. Offer the following prayer:

> God, our parent and protector,
> We come before you seeking the wisdom and the courage we need
> to confront the injustices we meet each day in our
> schools and communities.

Teach us the way to be your hands and your heart for people
  who are victims of injustice and whose voices are not heard.
We ask you to hear the petitions of your people as we say,
  "Lord, hear your people."

Invite the participants to respond with, "Lord, hear your people" after each petition you read:

○ For all soldiers fighting on foreign soil, we pray . . .
  For families living amid the terror and violence of war, we pray . . .
  For people who are treated with indifference and neglect, we pray . . .
  For those who work for peace and justice, we pray . . .
  For these and all the petitions we place before you, O God,
    we ask your blessing in the name of Jesus Christ, our
    Lord and savior.
  Amen.

Chapter 13

The Orange Drink

Key Themes

- We are called to care for others.
- We must see beyond labels and stereotypes.
- Service is a way of life for the Christian.

Scripture Connections

- Matthew 20:1–16 ("The last will be first, and the first will be last.")
- Matthew 25:31–40 (What you have done for my family, you have also done for me.)
- Mark 9:33–37 (Whoever receives another in my name receives me.)
- Philemon 8–21 ("Welcome him as you would welcome me.")

The Story

You will want to purchase a generic bottle of orange soda, along with a few bottles of name-brand soft drinks, and place them in a prominent location in the gathering space. Offer the following introduction before telling the story:

> ○ This story presents a simple symbol of the invisible faces that we may see every day—people who are longing for friendship, attention, or even a smile. God calls us to be ever aware of those around us, to be sensitive to their needs, to be open and welcoming, to be more Christlike.

As I was preparing for the final youth meeting of the year, I began to stock the refreshment table with soft drinks and snacks. One bottle of soda caught my eye as I placed it on the counter. This particular orange drink was one of the off brands, and it looked suspiciously familiar. It seemed as if I had placed this same orange drink on the table for each of the last several meetings and then returned it untouched to the cabinet afterward. Instead of throwing it away, I left it in its place. As the teens streamed in and began filling the chairs and floor space for class, I watched as they went for the snacks. Once again, the bottle of generic orange soda was ignored.

As class time approached, I also noticed the room was not quite as full as it was at the beginning of the year. Perhaps some of those missing were one-time visitors, forced by their parents to show up. Others had just drifted away over the course of the year as often happens. Regardless, quite a few were missing as compared to our first gathering several months earlier. After an opening prayer, I asked the group if they noticed anything about the beverages that had been set out. Some of them looked at me like I was crazy. Finally, one of the boys mentioned the orange drink. He had noticed it before.

After several looks of puzzlement, I decided to tell the class why I had asked the question. Every month they walked up to the snack table and pushed right past the plain, no-name brand of orange soda to get to the Pepsi, Dr. Pepper, Coca-Cola, or Mountain Dew — all the popular drinks. Not one person bothered to try the generic orange soda, not even one sip. Worse yet, most of the people in the room did not even remember the orange drink being there before.

Then I asked the group to think back to the first class in September. "Remember all those people who used to sit over here?" I asked as I gestured to an empty area on the floor. "Those people are like the orange drink. Every meeting many of us would go right by without even speaking to them, because we were in such a hurry to meet up with our friends and have fun. Imagine . . . some of them sat right in the middle of us, just like the orange soda sits with the Dr. Peppers and the Pepsis." Sure enough, as I listed the names of a few of the missing participants, the group members realized they did not even recall some of these people. Our church and youth community was fairly small, so this was a shock. I asked them to think of times when they felt left out or excluded. I noted that when we are in a large-group setting with many unfamiliar faces, we often tend to cling to the people we know. Yet somewhere in the room may be an "orange drink" — a person waiting to be noticed, thirsting for acknowledgment. I suggested that each of us take the time to notice others, to get past the labels and the exteriors and find out what is on the inside.

After our discussion, a couple things happened. First, that orange soda was opened and everyone had to have a little sip. There was no saving it for the next meeting — the group made sure of that. Sharing the orange drink was a demonstration that the lesson would be taken to heart. It represented a commitment to be more attentive to others. We may not be as popular as the others, but we just want someone to notice us, to care enough to give us a chance.

Second, it changed forever the way many of us look at orange sodas. Occasionally, by coincidence (or is it really?), there is an orange soda on the table at a gathering. It reminds us that there might be other "orange drinks" in the room. So we take a sip and seek those people out.

Reflecting on the Story

Depending on the number of participants, you may want to create small groups to discuss these questions. Be sure to provide adequate discussion time before bringing the participants back into a large-group setting for overall feedback and response. Another option would be to provide the participants with journals and invite them to write their responses.

- Describe a situation when you felt left out. In what group settings do you feel most comfortable? least comfortable?
- Recall the last time you were in a setting with others you did not know. Did you reach out to others, or were you more like the orange drink?
- Reflect on the last time you noticed someone new at school or church. What steps did you take to get to know that person? What could you have done differently to make that person feel more welcome?
- Jesus says, "Feed the hungry." How have you fed the hungry in your life? Recall how you may have fed someone with kindness rather than food.
- What situations have you encountered that make it difficult to reach out to others? How can peer pressure hold you back? What other pressures hold you back? How can you overcome those pressures and help others do the same?

Breaking Open the Message of the Story

Preparation

The following activities will assist the participants in breaking open the message of the story. Choose activities that are most appropriate for the group gathered and the time allotted.

Gather these items:

○ copies of *The Catholic Youth Bible*™ or another Bible, one for each small group of three or four

○ two sheets of newsprint

○ a marker

Get to Know Someone

Ask the participants to line up in the order of their birthdays. Then divide the group into pairs, pairing up participants that have the closest birthdays. Allow 10 minutes for each pair to talk and discover something they do not know about each other. Be prepared to assist by offering suggestions on topics for discussion if your group is well acquainted. For example, ask the participants to share about their greatest personal accomplishments, their dream jobs, or their favorite role models. Then have all the participants share with the large group what they learned about their partners.

"Orange Drink People"

Divide the large group into small groups of three or four. Give each group a Bible and ask the group members to search for "orange drink people" in the Scriptures. For groups who are not as familiar with the Bible, you might consider suggesting they search just the Gospels. Allow the groups 15 to 20 minutes to find a story (or person) and prepare an explanation to share with the large group. When the large group regathers, invite each small group to offer its presentation.

Welcoming Someone New

Within the large group, brainstorm ideas on how to make new people feel welcome. On a sheet of newsprint, list ideas as the group comes up with them. Ask specifically for good conversation starters that can be used to make a new person feel welcome. After the participants share their ideas, ask for a volunteer to role-play the part of a new person joining the group, and let the remaining participants attempt to make that person feel welcome. Afterward, ask the participants for any reaction to their part in the activity.

Welcome Packet

Invite the participants to brainstorm what they would include if they were creating a welcome packet for new church or group members. Jot down their ideas on a sheet of newsprint. Then, at a later time (or event), after you have created or collected these items, create the packets and devise a plan to distribute them to new members. Consider including a small bottle of orange soda!

Living the Story

Offer the following ideas to the participants as a way to continue the message of the story beyond the gathering. You might do this by listing all the ideas on a handout and sending it home, choosing one or two ideas to share and discuss with the participants, or listing the ideas on newsprint for review or discussion.

- Look around the room. Are there individuals here you really do not know? Resolve to get to know a little more about one person before the next gathering.
- Look in your own home. If you have a younger sibling or other family member that perhaps you do not acknowledge or spend enough time with, plan a special activity or outing with him or her. Make every effort to let this person know he or she is special and loved.
- The next time you are in an unfamiliar situation and feeling left out, find someone who feels the way you do and start a conversation.
- Get involved. Find a service organization and do some volunteer work. Truly feed the hungry by working at a soup kitchen. Clothe the naked by collecting clothes for the Red Cross or another organization. Make a difference!

Praying the Story

Preparation

Gather these items for the following prayer experience:

- ○ a table
- ○ a candle and matches
- ○ a copy of *The Catholic Youth Bible*™ or another Bible
- ○ a large bottle of generic orange soda
- ○ paper cups, one for each participant

Process

1. Prepare a prayer space in the center of the room. On a table, place a lit candle, a Bible, and any other symbolic objects meaningful to the participants. Also place the orange soda and the cups on the table.

2. Ask the participants to join you in the prayer space by forming a circle around the prayer table. Distribute a cup to each participant.

3. Offer the following comments in your own words:

○ There are many people in the world who are in need at this moment. Many do not have food to eat, clothes to wear, or a decent place to live. Others are sick and in need of healing and comfort. But for many, the need is to be loved. Many people hunger for companionship and acceptance. Tonight we will pray for those individuals who are in need of friendship, acceptance, and love.

Then offer the following prayer:

○ Loving and gracious God,
    we come to you tonight to ask for your guidance.
Give us the strength and courage to follow the example of
    your Son, Jesus.
May we always care for those around us
    and take the time to reach out and do our best to make our homes,
    our schools, our church, and our community a loving and
    welcoming place.
We pray this in your name.
Amen.

4. Tell the participants that they are invited to come forward to the prayer table, one at a time, and pour a small amount of orange soda into their cups. After they have done so, they may return to their places.

5. Once all the participants have a cup of orange soda, offer the following prayer:

> ○ Good and loving God,
>> As we share this drink,
>> we pray that everyone here today feels welcome.
> We pray that newcomers to our community will be welcomed
>> with open arms.
> We pray that new students will find acceptance at school.
> We pray that new members of our church will feel at home.
> We pray that all who are in need of love will find it.
> And we pray that we will all be part of bringing love, friendship,
>> and acceptance to all we meet.
> We ask all these things in the name of your Son, Jesus Christ,
>> who always reached out to those in need.
> Amen.

6. Invite everyone to raise their cups and then drink their share of the soda. Finally, conclude by asking the participants to think about how they can live out the message of the orange drink in the next few days. Ask them to make their best effort to fulfill that commitment.

Chapter 14

A Miracle

Key Themes

- As Christians, we believe in the power of prayer.
- God can accomplish all things.
- Sometimes God answers our prayer but not in the way we expect or the way we want.
- We must trust in God even when we do not understand.

Scripture Connections

- Psalm 37:4–6 (God will give you the desires of your heart.)
- Proverbs 3:4–6 (Trust in the Lord.)
- Matthew 21:21–22 (You will receive what you ask for.)
- John 11:38–44 (Jesus raises Lazarus from the dead.)

The Story

Offer the following introduction before telling the story:

  o   To pray for a miracle takes not only faith but also courage. Courage is needed to face the possibility that our prayer may not be answered. In this story, a son's faith is tested as he seeks to understand the reason God "ignored" his prayer.

My father went into the hospital on February 13. It was a Tuesday. I left work that day and met my brother at the emergency room. We were told that Dad had gotten a bug that made him very sick. With some antibiotics, a full recovery was expected, but it would take awhile. I remember Daddy looking at the doctor and holding up three fingers, saying, "Three days." That was how long he expected to be there.

Three days came and went with no improvement. In fact, Daddy seemed to be getting worse every day. The IV fluid did not seem to help, and he was eating and drinking little. Worse yet, he was very uncomfortable, and we could do little to help.

I remembered him sitting in my den just a few days earlier, in front of the fire. He was hoarse from a continuing sore throat. In spite of his whispers, he joined in a game of Jeopardy with me, my son, and a friend. Daddy did not fare too well in the first game, but he had a good time. In the second game, however, the categories were more to his liking. We all sat in amazement as he whispered answer after answer and continued to accumulate play money. I was so proud that although he was sick, his mind was still sharp.

Now, as I put Jeopardy on the television in the hospital room, there was no one to play along. Daddy's condition made watching television a chore. What we first thought to be a bug turned into something worse. By the next Monday, we were being told that his heart was weakening fast. His long-range prospects were poor. For the first time, we realized that even his short-range prospects were not good. Tuesday was yet another bad day—still no improvement, no rest, no eating, and only rare moments when we could glimpse the beautiful man inside the body that now betrayed him.

After leaving the hospital Tuesday evening, I went to a meeting at church. Standing outside in the parking lot after the meeting, I got a strong feeling of dread. I realized the next day would be Ash Wednesday, the beginning of Lent. For Catholics Lent is both a wonderful and a difficult time of year. It is difficult because we are called upon to sacrifice, to try to renew ourselves by denying our physical needs. It is also a beautiful time for reflection, for doing good deeds, and for contemplating the mystery of the Resurrection. This night I told my wife that tomorrow would be the day. We had not been given any indication, but I strongly felt my father would leave us on Ash Wednesday.

I barely slept that night, and I woke up early the next morning. I read the paper and noticed a large picture with a caption that read "The Healing Nun." The article told the story of a nun who possessed the power of healing. This nun was in town and would be speaking across town on Ash Wednesday morning. Part of me wanted to go. Another part feared getting my hopes up and being disappointed. Yet I truly believed that Daddy could be healed, both by medicine and by the power of God. How would I feel if I did not go and Daddy died? How would I feel if I went and no miracle occurred? Would I blame God? the nun? All this churned through my mind as I got dressed.

For once in my life, I think I truly turned the decision over to God. As I got in my van, I prayed the rosary. In effect, I told Jesus to take the wheel, and if I ended up at church, that was where I should be. I guess I was not that surprised when Jesus got me in a terrific traffic jam. After all, he had not been on the interstate that much. We made our way to the church, and I rushed up the steps not knowing what to expect.

As I entered, I realized Mass was in progress, and I was thankful. I knew I would be at the hospital later and would not be able to attend Ash Wednesday services. Afterward, the healing nun spoke. There was no talk of healing or miracles, only of Lent. I tried to find her after the talk but was told by a priest that she had already gone to speak to the school children. He offered to deliver my request, which I had written down on a card. I explained my situation, and he listened compassionately and promised to pass the message on. Then he said a short prayer for my father and me. I felt a little better as I headed to work. At least I had tried.

About an hour later, my brother called to say that Daddy was improving and had eaten breakfast. This was amazing. All along we had been thinking that if Daddy would only eat, his strength would return and he would recover. Could this be true? I was excited but also fearful that my hopes would get too high. I had to see for myself, so I left for the hospital an hour earlier than my usual lunch visit.

Before I entered the room, I took a deep breath and asked a nurse in the hall how Dad was doing. Her face brightened as she told me he was better. He had eaten actual food, and all the nurses were happy. I opened the door to see Daddy sitting up in the chair. He looked like a new man. The nurse told me of the great happenings that morning, and I began to believe in miracles. Daddy was eating breakfast at almost the exact time the priest had offered his prayer.

Soon my aunt and uncle arrived, and they too beamed at the turn of events. I proudly told the story of my morning search for a miracle. We all waited until the lunch tray arrived, and, as promised, the nurse sat in front of Daddy and fed him. I knelt next to the chair watching every bite, every sip of milk. She even made him pick up his own milk carton. This was great! Finally, we saw improvement.

Before I left, I kissed Daddy on the cheek, and got right next to his ear and said, "I'm proud of you!" He looked me in the eye and said, "I'm proud of you." With tears of joy filling my eyes, and a heart full of new-found hope, I left the hospital.

Returning to work, I was like a new man. I told and retold my story. He ate lunch! Such a small thing, but it was so wonderful—a miracle for sure!

Then I got the call from my brother at the hospital. Daddy's blood pressure was dropping, and it seemed the end was imminent. How could this be? He was doing so well. I went into deep shock and did not know if I could make the drive. As I turned down the familiar streets and passed all the same buildings, I thought of the many days that I had driven this path. How I wished I could drive it many more days. But I knew this would probably be the last time.

As I entered the room, my fears were realized. Daddy was not alert. He had indeed slipped back. The entire family gathered in the room, and we wept and prayed. Our prayers were not being answered, and my anxiety increased. Daddy soon left us peacefully, just past noon. Our prayers for recovery had changed to prayers for peace.

Through the pain and tears, I thought about the cruel turn of events. Why were my hopes ever raised that Wednesday morning? What sort of cruel joke was that? Would I turn on God now that my miracle had failed? What would become of me?

I then realized God had answered my prayer for healing and my prayer for a miracle. Certainly, Daddy now has no suffering. He is healed. I also remembered the joy and hope Daddy gave me in those few hours that Wednesday morning. Those were special gifts to me and the others who were there. At least for a little while, hope still lived within us. I would not trade those hours for anything in the world.

My miracle brought me one other great treasure—a memory I will cherish forever. In that time, I heard the words that every son wishes to hear from his father—words that I wish I could hear again. But I am thankful that on this Ash Wednesday of despair, a loving father fighting for life turned his eyes to a son filled with fear, and said simply, "I'm proud of you."

Daddy, I am proud of you. Thank you for the miracle.

Reflecting on the Story

Depending on the number of participants, you may want to create small groups to discuss these questions. Be sure to provide adequate discussion time before bringing the participants back into a large-group setting for overall feedback and response. Another option would be to provide the participants with journals and invite them to write their responses.

- If you have suffered the loss of a loved one, try to describe your relationship with God during that time. What were your prayers?
- Reflect on your personal prayer life. How often do you pray? What types of prayers do you pray? How do you pray?

- Do you believe in prayer? Do you *really* believe in prayer? Reflect on prayers in your life that have been answered and some that have not. What can you make of God's plan in the answers to those prayers?
- Reflect on a particularly difficult time in your life. Discuss how the experience strengthened your faith when you overcame that adversity.

Breaking Open the Message of the Story

Preparation

The following activities will assist the participants in breaking open the message of the story. Choose activities that are most appropriate for the group gathered and the time allotted.

Gather these items:

O   pens or pencils, one for each participant

O   sheets of blank paper, two for each participant

O   copies of *The Catholic Youth Bible*™ or another Bible, one for each small group of three to five

Unanswered Prayers?

Divide the large group into smaller groups of three to five participants. Distribute the bibles and ask each small group to find an instance when God seemingly did not answer a prayer. Allow 10 to 15 minutes for each group to find a passage and attempt to discover what God's answer was. Refer to these or other passages if groups need assistance: Genesis, chapter 7; Genesis, chapter 22; Job, chapter 1; the Book of Jonah; Matthew 4:18–21; Matthew 14:1–12; Matthew 26:36–46. Give each group time to present its stories and discuss God's plan at work.

Being Thankful

Give each participant a pen or pencil and a piece of paper. Ask each person to reflect on the story and list five to ten things the author is thankful to God for (family, love, support, nurses, medicine, hospitals, religion, church, and so on). Allow 5 minutes for individual brainstorming and then lead a large-group discussion of what the participants discovered. Emphasize that even in times of sorrow and loss, there are many things to be thankful for.

Miracles

Direct the participants to pair up for this activity. Give each pair a pen or pencil and a blank sheet of paper and ask that they write "Miracles" at the top. They then list miracles they have witnessed. They can include events called miracles by the media, such as last-second sports victories. Ask the participants to share their lists and have a discussion on what really constitutes a miracle. (Realize that we may take for granted some of God's little miracles, and be sure to recognize those as they are listed.)

Living the Story

Offer the following ideas to the participants as a way to continue the message of the story beyond the gathering. You might do this by listing all the ideas on a handout and sending it home, choosing one or two ideas to share and discuss with the participants, or listing the ideas on newsprint for review or discussion.

- Believe in the power of prayer. Pray tonight with a sincere heart and be open to God's response.
- Recall in your mind the names and faces of family members and friends who have died. Pray for each one by name. Recall what you may have learned from each and try to put one of those lessons into practice this week.
- Console the grieving. The next time someone you know suffers a loss, make an extra effort to extend an act of kindness.
- Look for miracles. Be open to the minor miracles that God performs every day. Don't take things for granted. Look for God's hand at work each day.

Praying the Story

Preparation

Gather these items for the following prayer experience:

○   a table

○   a candle and matches

○   a copy of *The Catholic Youth Bible*™ or another Bible

Process

1. Place a candle in the center of the gathering space (or on a prayer table). Invite the participants to gather in the center of the room and form a circle around the candle as you light it. Remind the participants that they are in the holy presence of God. Then ask a volunteer to proclaim Matthew 18:19–20 and Matthew 7:7–11. Allow a few moments of silence to follow.

2. Tell the participants to join hands, close their eyes, and remain silent. Then offer the following prayer introduction:

○   O merciful God, we, your children, are gathered here with confidence and open hearts.
Please look favorably on the prayers we offer you now.

3. Invite the participants to share specific prayers aloud. Refer to the list below for suggested types of prayers. When prayers have been offered, ask the group to pray for the intentions silently and then conclude by saying, "Dear Father, we ask these prayers, both spoken and unspoken, in the name of our brother, your Son, Jesus Christ." Then move on to the next category.

• prayers for forgiveness
• prayers for strength and courage
• prayers for help in our daily lives
• prayers for those who are sick in mind and body
• prayers for our families
• prayers for our church community
• prayers in thanksgiving for God's many blessings and prayers answered

4. Conclude the session by inviting the participants to join in praying the prayer that Jesus taught us, the Lord's Prayer.

Acknowledgments